BEST PUB WALKS IN PEMBROKESHIRE

Laurence Main

Published by Sigma Leisure – an imprint of
Sigma Press, 1 South Oak Lane, Wilmslow, Cheshire SK9 6AR, England.

British Library Cataloguing in Publication Data
A CIP record for this book is available from the British Library.

ISBN: 1-85058-407-9

Typesetting and Design by: Sigma Press, Wilmslow, Cheshire.

Cover picture: from an original painting of the Griffin Inn, Dale, by Elizabeth Webber

Printed by: Manchester Free Press

Preface

Certain places sparkle with vitality. Perhaps the earth's energies converge on peninsulas, or maybe the endurance of the ancient rocks shines through. Whatever causes it, the once and future county of Pembrokeshire will stir you. Stunning coastal scenery, of course, is the rule in Britain's only coastal national park. Those who know only the Coast Path miss the enchanting interior of a land of mystery and magic.

The Preseli Hills in the northern part of Pembrokeshire offer open moorland littered with prehistoric monuments. The bluestones were taken from here to Stonehenge, while less tangible features such as a terrestrial zodiac have been discerned. 'As above, so below', with the link between heaven and earth strengthened by St Brynach's visions of angels on Carn Ingli.

Pilgrims have made their way for centuries to the city of St David in the far west. Some avoided a hazardous sea voyage by landing at St Ishmael's and following old tracks above St Bride's Bay. Somewhere about Newgale they crossed the Landsker. This invisible frontier divided the native Welsh from the English-speaking settlers who gave Pembrokeshire the reputation of being a 'Little England beyond Wales'. Conquest entailed the construction of castles and the old county has its fair share, including the birthplace of Henry Tudor at Pembroke's mighty castle.

The Tudor dynasty fulfilled the prediction that the red dragon of Wales would eventually triumph over the Saxons. Henry VII, who was a descendant of King Arthur and lived in exile in Brittany at the spot where the king ended his days as a saint, was steeped in Arthurian legend. It seems appropriate that he set foot on British soil on his way to victory at Bosworth in 1485 near St Anne's Head. There may well have been a beacon here in the days of Arthur. His son, Henry VIII, of course, restored the Church's freedom from Rome, echoing the state of the original Celtic Church.

Celtic saints abound, with the remote St Govan's Chapel perhaps being the spot where Arthur's Sir Gawain served at the last as a hermit. The industrial revolution made a token intrusion further up the coast near Saundersfoot, with a band of coal which stretched across towards Nolton Haven. In general, however, nature and spiritual values were to maintain supremacy. Today it is just the oil refineries of Milford Haven that blot the landscape.

Coal and oil did contribute to the growth of the tourist trade. Fishguard almost became a transatlantic port, while the iron way even found its way deep into the Preselis at Rosebush. Take the train where there is a service (it's useful for Narberth, Tenby, Pembroke and Haverfordwest). You can reach all the walks by bus, although you'd need to stay overnight in Crymych, where the pub does provide bed and breakfast accommodation, in order to complete the walk inbetween buses. Using local public transport will mean one less car on roads that were not intended for modern traffic.

Free timetable booklets are available in Tourist Information Centres and by post from the Highways & Transportation Dept, Dyfed County Council, Llansteffan Road, Carmarthen, Dyfed, SA31 3LZ. Tel: 0267 233333 ext. 4333. Pembrokeshire has been part of Dyfed (itself a reincarnation of the old kingdom) since 1974. Impending local government re-organisation promises the return of Pembrokeshire. Its area amounts to 614 square miles, of which 225 square miles are within the National Park.

Accommodation of all types is readily available, including a good network of youth hostels, while many pubs offer bed and breakfast.

Tourist Information Centres or National Park Visitor Centres are at:

Broad Haven (0437 781412), Cardigan (0239 613230), Fishguard (0348 873484), Haverfordwest (0437 763110), Kilgetty (0834 812175), Milford Haven (0646 690866), Narberth (0834 860061), Newport (0239 820912), Pembroke (0646 622388), St David's (0437 720392), Saundersfoot (0834 811411) and Tenby (0834 842402).

The main tourist offices are:

Pembrokeshire Coast National Park Dept, Information Officer, County Offices, Haverfordwest, SA61 1QZ. Tel: 0437 764591 ext. 5135. Dyfed County Council, Informtion Officer, County Hall, Carmarthen, SA31 1JP. Tel: 0267 233333 ext. 4007. SPARC (South Pembrokeshire Partnership for Action with Rural Communities), The Old School, Station Road, Narberth, Dyfed, SA67 8DU. Tel: 0834 860965.

Ordnance Survey 1:25,000 scale Pathfinder maps come into their own on these walks. Learn how to use them with a good compass. Practise with the routes in this book, then enjoy the freedom of making your own. There are enough paths to last a lifetime, so come back frequently to take small areas in depth each time, rather than attempting to do too much in a short time superficially. Learn to love the land and it will share its secrets with you.

Commonsense is required when out in the country. Don't leave it too late and find yourself walking in the dark. Be careful at all times on clifftop paths, while a torch and batteries are easily carried. Always wear good walking boots. Carry spare clothing, including an anorak. Tel: 0839 500414 for an all-year-round weather forecast for Dyfed and Powys, or 0834 812516 for a seasonal weather forecast service just for Pembrokeshire.

Laurence Main

CONTENTS

Introduction

Pembrokeshire   1
Useful Welsh words   6
Real Ale   9
Opening Hours   10
The Walks   10

The Walks

1. St Dogmael's   12

The White Hart (0239 612099)

$2^1/_4$ miles. Easy.

2. Abercych   16

The Penrhiw Inn (0239 87229)

$4^1/_2$ miles. Easy.

3. Fishguard 21
The Royal Oak (0348 872514)
11 miles. Moderate.

4. Dinas 29
The Ship Aground (03486 261)
4 miles. Moderate.

5. Newport 33
The Golden Lion (0239 820321)
6 miles. Strenuous.

6. Trefin 37
The Ship Inn, Trefin (0348 831445)
The Sloop Inn, Porth-gain (0348 831449)
5 miles. Moderate.

7. Casmael (Puncheston) 43
The Drovers' Arms (0348 881469)
$4^1/_2$ miles. Moderate.

8. Crymych 47
The Crymch Arms (0239 831435)
12 miles. Strenuous.

9. St David's 51
The Farmers' Arms (0437 720328)
6 miles. Easy.

10. Solva 56

The Ship Inn (0437 721247)

3 miles. Moderate.

11. Nolton Haven 60

The Mariners' Inn (0437 710469)

4 miles. Moderate.

12. Wolf's Castle 64

Wolfe Inn (0348 87662)

6 miles. Moderate.

13. Rosebush 68

Tafarn Sinc Preseli (0437 532214)

5 miles. Strenuous.

14. Llanddewi Velfrey 72

Parc-y-lan Inn (0834 860532)

3 miles. Moderate.

15. Little Haven 76

The Swan Inn (0437 781256)

3 miles. Moderate.

16. Haverfordwest 80

The Bristol Trader Inn (0437 762122)

5 miles. Easy.

17. Hook   **85**

The New Anchor Inn (0437 891343)

$3^1/_2$ miles. Easy.

18. Marloes   **89**

The Lobster Pot Inn (0646 636233)

7 miles. Moderate.

19. Robeston Wathen   **93**

The Bridge Inn (0834 860541)

$7^1/_2$ miles. Easy.

20. Narberth   **97**

The Angel (0834 860574)

6 miles. Moderate.

21. Llangwm   **101**

The Cottage Inn (0437 891494)

$3^1/_2$ miles. Moderate.

22. Dale   **105**

The Griffin Inn (0646 636227)

7 miles. Moderate.

23. Saundersfoot   **110**

Royal Oak Inn (0834 813675)

5 miles. Moderate.

24. Angle 114
Hibernia Inn (0646 641517)
4 miles. Easy.

25. Pembroke 118
Cromwell's Tavern (0646 682223)
6 miles. Moderate.

26. Manorbier 123
The Castle Inn (0834 871268)
$3^1/_2$ miles. Strenuous.

27. Tenby 127
Hope and Anchor (0834 842131)
6 miles. Moderate.

LOCATION MAP

N

Fishguard ●3

●6
Trefin

Ramsey
Island

●St David's

Solva
●10

Wolf's
Castle
●12

PEMBROKE

11
●Nolton Haven

Haverfordwest
●16

15 Little
●Haven

Skomer
Island

17
●
Hook

21●
Llangwm

Marloes
●18

Dale
22●

Skokholm
Island

24 Angle
●

25
●
Pembroke

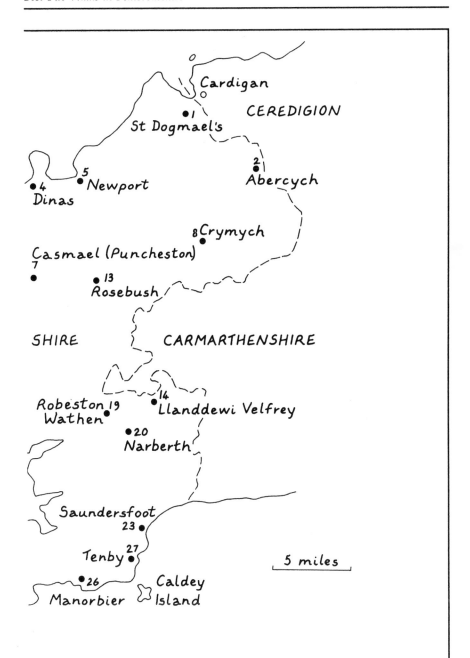

Introduction

The term 'Pembrokeshire' is recognized whatever the politicians and bureaucrats may decide for the south-western corner of Wales. The name conjures up visions of a beautiful natural landscape. Its bones are made up of very ancient rocks. In the north these are extremely old, going back 2000 million years, when Carn Ingli's peak above Newport was an active volcano. The earth's crust sank when the volcanic eruptions stopped. The sea came in and deposits of sediment on its bed formed the Cambrian rocks, whose layers can be seen on the south shore of Whitesand Bay. At a later stage (450 million years ago, in Ordovician times) the underwater volcanoes returned to life and the result is rhyolite, a lava as seen on the Preselis.

Warm coral seas covered southern Britain in Silurian times and fossils from its primitive marine creatures have been found near Marloes. Earth movements some 400 million years ago then created a highland zone formed of Old Red Sandstone. Wind, rain and ice have since worn these mountains down to the Preselis. The intense pressure on rocks that once formed an ocean bed was responsible for the delightful cliff scenery, as seen near Solva. Though the mountains rose to the north, the area around Milford Haven was a shallow sea. This abounded with life and the skeletal debris now composes the Carboniferous Limestone of South Pembrokeshire. Fast-flowing rivers in Upper Carboniferous times washed mud to the coast. Peat beds were formed and these were compressed into seams of coal. The lower beds contained the famous anthracite, as exposed near Saundersfoot.

Despite the fracturing and folding of Pembrokeshire's underlying rocks, the surface impression is of plateau and deeply-incised valleys. The former sea bed was raised in steps. When rain created rivers, they cut through the surface to form the valleys. the Ice Age has left few scars, allowing for the high rock surfaces being scratched by ice, the shattering of rocks into jagged peaks and some glacially-deposited erratic boulders. When the glaciers melted, however, river valleys were drowned by a rise in sea level, with Milford Haven a classic example. A smaller-scale example of such a ria is the harbour at Solva.

There are tales of lost lands under the waves and substance is given to these when submerged forests are revealed, as at Wiseman's Bridge. Folk memory may date from the Old Stone Age, when hunters are known to have roamed what was then the tundra of South Pembrokeshire. The Mesolithic or Middle Stone Age people of post-glacial times, from about 8000 BC, ranged more widely. Farming came with the Neolithic, or New Stone Age, around 4000 BC, when the sea level was much as it is now. Axe 'factories' must have been sited on the Preselis as the local stone was formed into axes which made their way around Neolithic Britain. Evidence of social organization also comes in the form of impressive stone tombs, known as cromlechs and dolmens. Even more mysterious is the presumed link between Pembrokeshire and Stonehenge, where the bluestones could only have come from the Preselis. Ingenious solutions to the problem of how they were transported to Wiltshire include logs and rafts, while some cling to the belief that a friendly glacier may have done the job during the Ice Age. Ancient myths abound, such as levitation of the stones. Perhaps science will rediscover the secrets of sonics. When you are surrounded by the haunting beauty of the Preselis, such speculation does not seem too far off the mark.

Not all the stones went to Stonehenge. A simpler stone circle stands at Gors Fawr, on the moorland less than one mile to the west of the hamlet of Mynachlog-ddu, to the south of Mynydd Preseli. Bedd Morris, above Newport, is an example of an isolated stone which may have waymarked an ancient track. These stones were erected around 2500 BC when the Bronze Age was beginning. The three cairns on Foeldrygarn, west of Crymych, are examples of the Bronze Age's conspicuous burial places.

The Iron Age was ushered in around 500 BC with the construction of hill-forts and other defensive measures, particularly the digging of ditches to form 'raths' or promontory forts. There must have been conflict with Celtic incomers. When the Romans reached here in the first century AD the inhabitants were known to them as the Demetae. Roman influence on Pembrokeshire appears to have been negligible and contact with Ireland was strong when the legions departed in 383 AD. Saints such as Brynach and, probably, Govan, were Irish. St David was British, however. His *llan* or sacred enclosure became the most important ecclesiastical centre in Wales.

The Vikings were attracted to Pembrokeshire's islands and coastline and ravaged St David's eight times before the Normans arrived in the 11th century. Force of arms gave South Pembrokeshire its English character, while Welsh is hardly spoken south of the imaginary frontier known as the Landsker. Manorbier blessed us with Giraldus Cambrensis, whose writings paint a vivid picture of medieval Welsh life. Pembroke Castle was the birthplace of Henry Tudor, the victor at Bosworth. His son, Henry VIII, united England and Wales with the Act of Union in 1536. The reign of Elizabeth I was distinguished by the life of George Owen of Henllys, author of the Description of Pembrokeshire. Then, as now, Pembrokeshire was noted for its bare, open, landscape subject to storms blowing from the sea.

South Pembrokeshire (the 'Little England beyond Wales') was rich and fertile, yielding the best grain in abundance. Lime and seaweed were available as fertilisers and much wheat and barley was exported. Cattle were pastured in the Welsh-speaking parts, around the hills. The county's third commodity was wool. There was no expense on fodder as snow never settled here for long. The wool was coarser than English wool but the flesh was considered highly desirable. Butter and cheese were also of economic importance. As well as wheat and barley, the English grew rye, peas and beans. The Welsh grew oats on their less fertile land. Haverfordwest boasted 'one of the greatest and plentifullest markets', while Pembroke and Tenby also had markets (a daily one for fish in Tenby). St David's and Newport had smaller scale markets for victuals.

Not all Pembrokeshire traders were legitimate. Smuggling was a way of life for many in the 17th and 18th centuries. Some deliberately wrecked passing ships by luring them with lights onto rocks. Others became notorious pirates, even if Bartholomew Roberts was a teetotal one. It seems hardly surprising that when the French set an invasion force ashore near Fishguard in 1797, they were routed by the local women led by Jemima Nicholas.

If the French had invaded in 1839 they might well have found the local population on their side. Agriculture was in the grip of a depression and the rural population was increasing. Improved roads were paid for by tolls. The local farmers who needed to cart lime through the toll-gate at Efail-wen on 13th May, 1839, decided they had suffered enough. They destroyed the gate and set fire to the toll-house. The gate was re-erected and protected by seven special constables but on 6th June,

1839, some 400 turned up wearing women's clothes and smashed the gate down again. The Daughters of Rebecca were in business. They succeeded in having most of their grievances removed by 1844. Their inspiration had been a Biblical text: 'And they blessed Rebekah, and said to her, may your descendants possess the gates of those who hate them'.

Biblical texts went down a treat in 19th century Wales. Religious enthusiasm was of the Nonconformist sort, resulting in the building of many independent chapels. Pride of place was given to the pulpit, from where legendary preachers could whip up 'hwyl' and send their congregations into ecstatic convulsions. The small tenant farmers who went to these chapels objected to having to pay tithes to the discredited Anglican clergy. Demonstrations and riots about this marked the 1880s.

The excess rural population were found employment in Pembrokeshire slate quarries in the latter half of the 19th century. Some of the slates for the Palace of Westminster were supplied by the Gilfach quarry on the southern slopes of Mynydd Preseli, at Llangolman. The slate industry was boosted by the arrival of the railway. One especially picturesque line served the Rosebush quarries. Their owner, Sir Hugh Owen, dreamed that it would bring tourists to this delightful area but the charms of Rosebush are still largely unknown. On the northern coast, at Porthgain, there was a harbour for the export of crushed stone. Its memorials lie in many metalled roads as well as public buildings in London, Dublin and Liverpool.

The sea is never far away in Pembrokeshire and it has brought hope of prosperity. The 1880s saw the prospect of Milford Haven capturing Liverpool's transatlantic trade. Lord Nelson had pronounced on the potential of its harbour to become the greatest commercial port on the west coast of Britain, in 1802. The urbane husband of his mistress Emma Hamilton, Sir William Hamilton, owned the land on which Milford Haven was founded late in the 18th century. In the event, the Admiralty established its dockyard just across the water at Pembroke, where the largest three-decker ship in the world, the *Duke of Wellington*, was launched in 1852. Milford Haven failed in its bid to rival Liverpool but it did acquire a large trawler fleet in the early 1900s, being ranked as the sixth largest fishing port in Britain. The fishing industry entered a rapid decline after its record catch of 59,286 tons was recorded in 1946 (boosted by the effects of World War II on the fishing-grounds).

As one door closed, another opened. The 1950s saw both BP and Esso choose Milford Haven as the port to accommodate their big new oil tankers. Its wide, sheltered, waterway can take vessels of up to 55ft draught even at low tide. The lack of silting problems meant that there would be no need for continuous dredging. Land was cheap, so the oil refineries soon appeared. Pride in becoming Britain's premier oil port may not endear these acres to the walker. Perhaps the sight may make some do without cars and turn to public transport to reach the starts of walks! North Sea oil has affected the importance of Milford Haven's refineries, of course, though the future holds the danger of oil being extracted from the Irish Sea. The oil industry and its attendant pollution is of particular concern to the wildlife for which Pembrokeshire is internationally renowned.

Ornithologists flock here for its sea birds, while casual visitors marvel at the carpets of flowers in spring. All sorts of birds find their way here from different directions, from across the landmass of Europe, at the eastern limit of the Atlantic and the warm Gulf Stream, or at the southern end of a range from the Arctic. The mild climate encourages plant growth, while most of the rain falls inland over the hills, rather than on the coast. The razorbill features on the emblem of the Pembrokeshire Coast National Park. A member of the auk family, it is especially strong on Elegug Stacks from May to July.

The off-shore islands are special havens for both birds and flowers. There are 35,000 pairs of Manx shearwaters during the breeding season on Skokholm, with perhaps 100,000 pairs of Skomer. You don't have to be a boat trip away from a coastal pub to savour special sights, however. A dolphin set up home in Solva harbour during the summer of 1985, while the thick undergrowth of the Daugleddau may conceal a tiny muntjac (the Chinese barking deer). Butterflies include the clouded yellow, the painted lady and the purple hairstreak. Primroses bloom early here to herald a succession of colourful flowers through the spring, from celandines to sea pinks, hawthorn and bluebells to red campion. Clover and ox-eye daisies are followed by dog roses and honeysuckle.

One endangered species in South Pembrokeshire has, for centuries, been the Welsh-speaker. North of the Landsker you can hear Welsh spoken and I experienced the most encouraging and patient shopkeeper in Fishguard who was glad to help me do my shopping in Welsh. When Pembrokeshire became part of Dyfed in 1974, the position of the Welsh-speakers was strengthened. Bilingual road signs can now be seen in such English bastions as Pembroke. An understanding of the Welsh language can do much to enhance your walking holiday here. Practice these pronunciations:

a	=	ah
c	=	k (hard)
ch	=	as in *loch*
dd	=	th in *the*
e	=	eh
f	=	v
ff	=	f
g	=	as in *go* (hard)
ngh	=	as in *anguish*
i	=	ee
ll	=	say l, keep tongue in this position and gently blow
o	=	oh
th	=	as in *through* (not as in *the*)
w	=	often as oo, with cwm (valley) sounding as coomb
y	=	as e in *the* (y or yr), or as i, so that Dyffryn sounds like *derffrin*

Some common place names use the following words:

aber	=	estuary, river-mouth or confluence
afon	=	river
bach, fash	=	small
bedd	=	grave
betws	=	chapel or oratory
blaen	=	head of the valley
bont, pont	=	bridge
braich	=	arm
brith	=	speckled
bryn	=	hill
bwlch	=	pass, defile
bychan	=	little
cadair	=	chair
cae	=	field
caer	=	fort
capel	=	chapel
carn, carnedd	=	pile of stones
carreg	=	rock
castell	=	castle
cau	=	deep hollow
cefn	=	ridge

celli, gelli	=	grove
ceunant	=	ravine
clogwyn	=	precipice
coch	=	red
coed	=	woodland
congl	=	corner
cors, gors	=	bog
craig	=	rock
crib	=	narrow ridge
croes	=	cross
cwm	=	valley
dinas	=	fort
dol, ddol	=	meadow
drws	=	door
dwr	=	water
dwy	=	two
dyffryn	=	valley
eglwys	=	church
eira	=	snow
esgair	=	mountain shoulder
fawr, mawr	=	big
felin, melin	=	mill
ffordd	=	road
ffridd	=	mountain pasture
ffynnon	=	well, spring
foel, moel	=	rounded hill
fynydd, mynydd	=	mountain
gam	=	crooked
glan	=	bank, shore
glas, las	=	blue, green
glyder	=	heap
glyn	=	glen
gwastad	=	plain, level ground
gwern	=	marsh
gwyn	=	white
gwynt	=	wind
hafod, hafotty	=	summer dwelling
hen	=	old
hendre	=	winter dwelling

hir	=	long
isa, isaf	=	lower
llan	=	sacred enclosure, church
llechwedd	=	hillside
llethr	=	slope
llwyd	=	grey
llwyn	=	grove
llyn	=	lake
maen	=	stone
maes	=	field
morfa	=	coastal marsh
mur	=	wall
nant	=	brook, stream
newydd	=	new
oer	=	cold
ogof	=	cave
oleu	=	light
pant	=	small hollow
pen	=	head, top
penrhyn	=	promontory
pentre, pentref	=	village
pistyll	=	spout, cataract
plas	=	mansion
pwll	=	pool
rhaeadr	=	waterfall
rhiw	=	hill
rhos	=	moorland, marsh
rhyd	=	ford
sarn	=	paved way, causeway
sych	=	dry
tal	=	end
tan	=	under
tarren	=	hill
tir	=	land
tomen	=	mound
traeth	=	stretch of shore
tre	=	town, hamlet
tri	=	three
trwyn	=	nose, promontory

twll	=	hole
ty	=	house
tyddyn	=	smallholding
ucha, uchaf	=	upper
uwch	=	above
waun	=	moor
y	=	the, of the
yn	=	in
ynys	=	island
ysgol	=	school, ladder
ysgubor	=	barn
ystrad	=	valley floor, strath

If you can say nothing else, do try these:

| Good morning | = | Bore da (bor-eh-da) |
| Thank you | = | diolch (dee-olc) |

Real Ale

Wales is the home of real water, which can be drunk straight from the tap and, indeed, St David was known as the water-drinker. Some Welsh water, such as Cerist mineral water from near Dinas Mawddwy, is bottled and sold in England.

Wales is famous for its brewing history and there is the Celtic link with whisky (there is a distillery today in Brecon). Nonconformist conscience may have persuaded many to stick to tea, but tea has nothing to do with Wales, while the tea plantations in countries like Sri Lanka exploit cheap local labour and deprive them of land to grow valuable food on. Ale is a more traditional drink than beer and it was traditionally drunk because it was safer than water. Ale in the Middle Ages was thick, sticky and sweet. Hops weren't introduced until the 15th century, adding preservative qualities as well as bitterness and flavour. Sugar was later added to the list of ingredients (water, barley, hops, yeast and sugar). Welsh beers should be every bit as good as English ones, even though there are not as many Real Ales to choose from. The quality of the local water enhances beer brewed in Wales, so do try the local brews.

Each of the pubs in this book serves real ale on draught. This means that the beers are still fermenting when they leave the brewery. This is known as secondary fermentation because it supplements the primary fermentation which took place in the brewery's large brewing vessels. The process continues at a slow pace as the barrels are racked in the pub cellar. Carbon dioxide is produced and escapes through a spile hole. The thirsty walker may receive gravity drawn beer, direct from the barrel, or beer from a hand pump or electric pump attached to the bar. Apart from this pumping, real ale is free of the carbon dioxide or nitrogen used to force pasteurised varieties (where the fermentation has been killed off) under pressure out of their kegs. These gassy beers are the ones that need the glossy adverts. They are shunned by lovers of traditional ales. Many landlords take a different view, however. Traditional real ale is less easy to keep and great care has to be taken regarding temperature and cleanliness. The draught beer has a very short 'shelf-life' and it takes skill, acquired from both training and experience, to serve a good pint of real ale.

Opening Hours

Under recent legislation pubs in England and Wales can now open for a maximum of 12 hours each day on Mondays to Saturdays (being 11 am to 11 pm) and for $6^1/_2$ hours on Sundays (being noon to 3 pm and 7 pm to 10.30 pm) unless extensions have been granted by local licensing magistrates. Most country pubs do not find it in their interest to take full advantage of the 'relaxed' hours during the week and tend to stick to the 'traditional' hours of noon to 3 pm and 6 pm to 11 pm or 7 pm to 11 pm. Check each pub individually.

The Walks

Each walk in this book follows rights of way to which you, as a member of the public, have unrestricted access. Should you come across any problems, send full details (including grid references) to the Welsh Officer of the Ramblers' Association, Ty'r Cerddwyr, High Street, Gresford, Wrexham, Clwyd, LL12 8PT, tel. 0978 855148.

The walks are numbered in sequence (almost) from north to south and are spread all over Pembrokeshire. Use the Ordnance Survey Path-finder maps as detailed for each walk. They are marvellous keys to the countryside and an investment in them will be repaid many times over as you progress to inventing your own routes. The walks average just over five miles each in length and range from $2^1/_4$ miles to 12 miles. Route 17 (Hook) and 21 (Llangwm) can be linked together to form a 9 mile walk.

All walks should be within the capabilities of anyone of average fitness. Allow about 1 hour for every 2 miles. Allow plenty of time to enable the walk to be completed in daylight. Cliff-top paths, in particular, are not the best places to be caught out at dusk. Even in daylight they should be treated with respect: children should be warned and dogs controlled. Keep to the path and treat it as a privilege to walk across someone else's land; in that way we can build an atmosphere of co-operation, rather than confrontation, in the countryside.

The Country Code

❏ Guard against all risk of fire

❏ Fasten all gates

❏ Keep dogs under proper control

❏ Avoid damaging fences, hedges and walls

❏ Keep to paths across farm land

❏ Leave no litter

❏ Safeguard water supplies

❏ Protect wildlife, wild plants and trees

❏ Go carefully on country roads

❏ Respect the life of the countryside.

1. St Dogmael's

Route: St Dogmael's – Y Felin – Abbey Ruins – Cwn Degwel -Pencnwc – Ysgubor-hen – St Dogmael's.

Distance: 2¼ miles. Easy.

Map: OS Pathfinder 1010 (Cardigan & Dinas Head).

Start: The White Hart, St Dogmael's (SN 165460).

Access: St Dogmael's is on the B4546 just across the river (Afon Teifi) and one mile to the west of Cardigan. There is a car park in the village (marked on the map) as well as the car park for patrons opposite the pub. The bus shelter near the pub is served by buses numbers 407 (from Cardigan on weekdays) and 409 (Tuesdays only, Cardigan-Molygrove). There is an excellent youth hostel at Poppit Sands, which is served by bus no 407 (extended route) in July and August only. Many more buses run to Cardigan.

The White Hart, St Dogmael's (0239 612099)

Medieval monks drank so much alcohol here that their abbot had to ban one from drinking any more, as well as cautioning others. This notorious den of ill-repute was also a brothel, so watch out! No food is served (is any needed with so much else on offer?), but there's plenty of real ale. There is also rumoured to be a ghost. Opening hours are 11 am to 3 pm and 6 pm to 11 pm on weekdays, noon to 3 pm and 7 pm to 10.30 pm on Sundays.

St Dogmael's

The mill (Y Felin) was first recorded as a corn mill in the 1640s. While there is a record of a fulling mill (for cloth) in 1291, the name of the road between this mill and the abbey ruins is Shin Grug (husk of wheat) so perhaps corn has been ground here since the days of the monks. Sadly, the mill was left derelict after the second world war. Life was restored to it in 1980, when a new owner started to refurbish it. The attractive mill pond was cleared of debris and re-flooded in 1981. Guided tours are available, while the wholemeal flour produced here and bread baked with it are usually for sale. An adjoining tea-room also offers refreshments. Enjoy these on the patio overlooking the water-wheel. The mill and tea-room are open daily throughout the summer between 10.30 pm and 5.30 pm (except Saturdays and Sunday mornings). The mill is open on weekdays from 9.30 am to 5 pm during the winter, while Sunday lunches may be available in the tea-room. Telephone – 0239 613999

St Dogmael was a Celtic saint who lived around AD500. A link with that period is provided by the memorial stone now kept in the parish church. Inscribed in both Latin and Ogham (early Irish), it reads 'Sagranus the son of Cvnomatvs'.

The Normans brought monks here in 1115 and the monastery became an abbey in 1120. Fine buildings were erected but the spiritual character fo the place seemed to suffer as a consequence. Much of the stone was plundered after the Dissolution, although the north and west walls still indicate their previous glory.

The Mill Pond

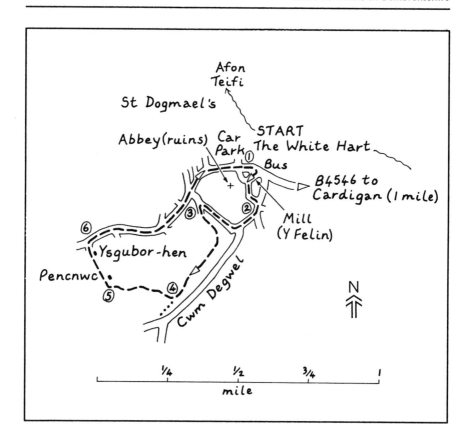

The Walk

1. Go left and turn right to cross the road and pass the pub car park on your right. Continue past the mill (Y Felin) on your left and the abbey ruins on your right (visit the church to see the Ogham stone). Come to a T-junction and turn right to pass Mwtshwr on your left. Bear right at a fork to head towards Cwm Degwel.

2. Fork right along a narrow, lower, road which is signed 'unsuitable for motor vehicles'. Turn right with this to admire the view over thee abbey ruins and the Teifi estuary on your right.

3. Turn sharply left along a No Through Road. At its end, continue along a signposted public footpath which overlooks the steep-sided valley of Cwm Degwel on your left. Keep close to the wall on your right!

4. Turn right through a kissing-gate and walk with a hedge on your right to a gate giving access to an enclosed footpath. This is the right of way but it may be overgrown. The farmer's wife (at Pencnwc) assured me that walkers who chose to walk in the field to the right of and above the path were tolerated (use the gates, leaving them as you find them).

5. When level with the farm buildings of Pencnwc on your right and when the enclosed path reaches a corner, turn right through a gate in that corner to walk along the right-hand edge of a field, behind the farmhouse (according to the lady at Pencnwc) and through a gate to join the farm's access track. Go ahead along this and pass Ysgubor-hen on your right.

6. Turn right along the road back into St Dogmael's and the White Hart, which will appear on your left.

2. Abercych

Route: Penrhiw – Abercych – Forestry Commission Cenarth -Penrhiw.

Distance: 4½ miles. Easy.

Map: OS Pathfinder 1011 (Newcastle Emlyn).

Start: The Penrhiw Inn, Abercych (SN 250403).

Access: Abercych is served by the B4332 road about two miles south-west of its junction with the A484 at Cenarth. Buses (numbers 460 and 461) run to Cenarth on their way between Cardigan and Carmarthen via Newcastle Emlyn.

The Penrhiw Inn, Abercych (0239 87229)

This hamlet's old pub was demolished in the 1980s and the old post office was extended to replace it around 1988. Bed and breakfast accommodation is available, as are real ale and food. Despite its lack of years, this pub does have an authentic ghost. The landlord's bedroom door opens onto what was an old stable block and the landlord has seen the ghost of Dai, who used to look after the horses there, wearing a coaching jacket. The landlady has often felt a cold presence by that door. The corner occupied by this pub is a notorious black-spot for road accidents, with 10 lorries overturning into the pub car park in less than 6 years. Watch where you park your car!

Opening hours are 11 am to 11 pm on weekdays, noon to 3 pm and 7 pm to 10.30 pm on Sundays. More restricted opening hours may operate during the winter.

Abercych

Yes, alright I did wander across the border into old Carmarthenshire on this route, but I was enjoying myself too much on the old green lane and taking too much care of the border with Ceredigion to the north of the

Turn right at the ford to reach the footbridge

Afon Teifi to notice that Cararthenshire lay on the eastern side of the
Afon Cych. It's all Dyfed anyway and it's the ancient Kingdom of Dyfed
that counts here because we are in the world of *The Mabinogion*. Here is
where Pwyll, Lord of Dyfed, went hunting and met Arawn King of
Annwn (the Underworld).

Perhaps the ford encountered in this walk is the ford where Pwyll had to
appear in Arawn's likeness and deal with Hafgan. First, Pwyll had to go
to Annwn and sleep with Arawn's wife. He managed to be tender and
pleasant to her for a year during the day, then to turn his back on her
every night. When the year was up, Pwyll killed Hafgan with one blow.
After uniting Hafgan's Kingdom with that of Arawn he was able to
return to the Cych valley and change places with Arawn. When the real
Arawn went to bed with the Queen, she received a pleasant surprise. His
wife showed such amazement that Arawn soon realised how well his
friend had behaved and from then on Pwyll and Arawn were the
strongest of allies. As you continue along the old track on the Carmarthenshire side of the ford, consider just how ancient it may be and who
could have followed it.

The Walk

1. Turn right along the road through the linear hamlet of Abercych. Pass
   the old school on your left, then turn right down a No Through Road.
   This metalled lane leads to a ford in the Afon Cych.

2. Turn right as you approach the ford and follow a footpath through a
   kissing-gate and over a footbridge across the river. Bear left to pass a
   house on your right, then turn right along a hedged track. Bear right
   at a fork at the foot of a wooded slope and pass above the house on
   your right.

3. Follow a delightful old cart track which has a bare rock surface. This
   climbs above the wooded slope as it bears left, overlooking the Afon
   Teifi on your left. Eventually this track turns right to a junction near
   the farm buildings of Penlan-Cenarth.

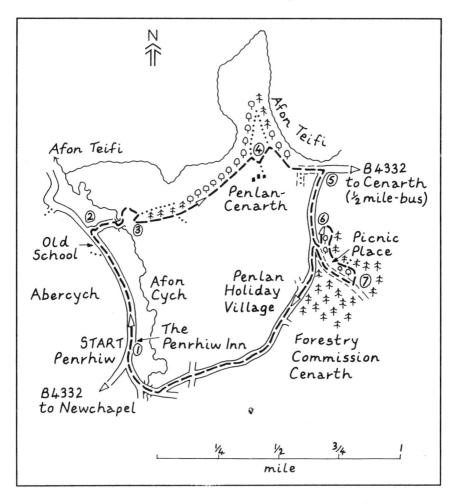

4. Ignoring the field gate on your left, bear left, away from Penlan-Cenarth. Turn right at the next track junction to descend with a steep, wooded, slope descending to the Afon Teifi on your left. Pass a concrete farm lane on your right as you go ahead down to the B4332 road.

5. Turn right along the B4332 to reach the Forestry Commission's Cenarth wood on your left. Turn left at its entrance to walk above a stream on your right. Go down steps with a wooden handrail.

6. Turn right across a footbridge and fork left to reach a wooden rail. Bear right with it on your left. Climb through broad-leaved woodland, then with conifers on your left, to a picnic place. Bear left through a kissing-gate and bear left at the first fork, then right at the second. Bear right to a path junction.

7. Turn right to walk with conifers on your left and broad-leaved trees on your right. Continue back down to the B4332 road and go left along it, passing Penlan Holiday Village on your right. Ignore a road on your left, then a lane on both sides. Cross a bridge over the Afon Cych to bear right uphill and head back to the pub.

3. Fishguard

Route: Fishguard – Goodwick – Pembrokeshire Coast Path -Carregwastad Point – Llanwnda – Goodwick – Fishguard.

Distance: 11 miles. Moderate.

Map: OS Pathfinder 1032 (Fishguard).

Start: Royal Oak, Fishguard (SM 958371).

Access: If you come by train or boat to Fishguard, join this route in Goodwick. You could also shorten it by taking bus no. 410 to Goodwick from Fishguard. The start of the walk is served by buses numbers 411 (from St David's) and 412 (Haverfordwest-Cardigan). Being an Irish ferry port, Fishguard is easy to reach by car, at the end of the A40.

The Royal Oak, Fishguard (0348 872514)

The famous surrender which ended the French farce of 1797 was signed here. One room of the pub is devoted to relevant memorabilia, including a French musket and Jemima Nicholas' warning bell. The pub itself dates from the Middle ages, although the only rumoured ghost is that of the great Jemima, 'Jemima Fawr', who was the heroine of the hour. A cobbler said to be able to beat any man in Fishguard in a fight, she single-handedly captured a dozen of the French invaders.

Real ale, food and bed and breakfast accommodation are all available. Opening hours are 11 am to 11 pm on weekdays during the high season, otherwise 11 am to 3 pm and 6 pm to 11 pm, plus noon to 3 pm and 7 pm to 10.30 pm on Sundays.

The French Farce

Historians have failed to take seriously the invasion by a French army at this point in 1797. The facts are these:

The French believed that the oppressed peasants were ready to rise up against the English crown. To help them do this a lugger, a corvette and two frigates slipped out of Brest on 17th February, 1797. On board were 1400 men each with 100 rounds of ammunition and four days' rations of food and double brandy. They should have landed at Bristol, but a sighting of the Dublin packet boat frightened them and they ended up here. This may not have been by chance. One of the invaders was James Bowen from a farm near Carregwastad. He had been transported for horse-stealing and either took the chance of a passage home or intended malice against his former employer. This wasn't the french Foreign Legion but the Black Legion, complete with black arm-bands. Most of the soldiers were convicts and their leader was an Irish-American, Colonel Tate.

The ships, flying British flags, were sighted off St David's and easily recognised as French. This explains why the alarm was raised so quickly. They were prevented from landing at Fishguard by a single shot from the fort, so they went to Carregwastad Point (out of sight) and disembarked on a calm, moon-lit night after the initial landing at 5 pm on 22nd February, 1797. The next morning saw them commanding the heights of Garnwnda and the ships sailed back to Brest. The French soon began knocking up the local peasants and found to their great delight that everybody was well-supplied with Portuguese wine from a shipwreck in January. As they drank it, Lord Cawdor gathered 575 men from the Yeomanry Cavalry, the Pembroke Company of Gentlemen, the Fishguard Fencibles, the Cardigan Militia and some Royal Navy sailors. The stars of the show were the women, whose red cloaks and hats (not, it seems, the top hats for which Wales became famous in the 19th century) made them resemble soldiers from a distance. Jemima Nicholas, the cobbler from Fishguard, wielded a pitch-fork with effect and by the afternoon of 24th February all the invaders had surrendered, laying down their arms on the beach near the A40 between Goodwick and Fishguard. Some were still paralysed with drink and unable to move when Colonel Tate signed the document of surrender at the Royal Oak Inn, Fishguard. Eight of the invaders had drowned coming ashore while another 12 were killed in some fighting. One Welsh woman was killed whilst a pistol was being loaded in a pub. The monument on Carregwastad Point was erected to mark the centenary of the event in 1897.

The Royal Oak

Fishguard

The film version of Dylan Thomas' *Under Milk Wood* was made here, while the Royal National Eisteddfod has been held here in 1936 (when the stones of the Gorsedd Circle encountered at direction point 2 were erected) and in 1986.

The harbour village, Goodwick, was built at the start of the 20th century to house railway and port workers. A project to develop Fishguard as a harbour for transatlantic liners during the mid-19th century was delayed by the Irish potato famine. Revived by the Great Western Railway in 1899, two million tons of rock blasted from Goodwick's cliffs were used to make the North Breakwater. A railway terminus was opened in the floor of the quarry in 1906. Transatlantic liners started to use the port, which was 40 miles nearer New York than Liverpool. Three or four special trains were required for each boat, with the Booth Line using the port from 1908 to 1914, Cunard between 1909 and 1914 and the Blue Funnel Fleet from 1910 to 1912. It wasn't the Great War that stopped these services but the building of the East Breakwater in 1913. Silting caused by this made it impossible for the bigger ships, like the *Mauritania*, to tie up at the quay-side. Fishguard also lacked Liverpool's industrial hinterland. The ferry service to Rosslare, in Ireland, remains.

Shipping had long used this bay. One merchant ship was seized by the buccaneer John Paul Jones' vessel *Black Prince* during the American War of Independence. He demanded 500 guineas ransom and fired two broadsides on Fishguard, one of which injured the sister of the author Richard Fenton.

A lifeboat was first stationed here in 1822. Needle Rock, across the bay, marks the wreck of the *Hermina*, a three masted Dutch motor schooner. Taking shelter here in a strong gale in December 1920, she dragged her anchor and summoned the Fishguard lifeboat *Chapter-house* with distress flares. Despite the tremendously difficult seas, seven of the ten crew were rescued. At one point the lifeboat was lifted by the waves onto the ship's rigging. The captain, chief officer and second mate chose to stay on board, despite pleas from the lifeboat, which had to be rowed back to the quay-side because its engine was severely drenched and refused to start, while the wind had ripped its mizzen sail to pieces. After completing the hazardous three-hour trip, more flares were seen from the

Hermina. The only hope now was a cliff rescue. The second mate was drowned as the vessel broke apart upon hitting Needle Rock, but the other two were saved by William Morgan when he was lowered by rope to the base of the cliff. The rescuers were rewarded with watches by the Dutch government.

Pen Anglas

Pen Anglas is famous for its jointed five-sided columns in cross-section through the dolerite. This is the Welsh version of the Giant's Causeway in Northern Ireland and Fingal's Cave in Scotland.

Llanwnda

St Gwyndaf, to whom the church is dedicated, was a sixth-century Celtic Saint from Brittany. Asser, the friend of England's King Alfred the Great, was educated here, while Giraldus Cambrensis (see the Manorbier Walk, No. 26) was a rector in the 12th century. The church has a Celtic bellcote tower, plus a lepers' squint in the porch. A neolithic burial chamber was sited on the nearby crags of Garnwnda.

The Walk

1. Go right, down West Street. Turn right along Penslade, as signposted for the Gorsedd Circle.

2. Continue along the cliff top path, keeping the sea on your right. Waymarked in blue as The Marine Walk, the path goes down steps and turns left around Saddle Point.

3. Turn right down steps to the A40 and walk between the road and the beach towards Goodwick. Cross the railway and turn left at a T-junction, almost immediately turning sharply right up New Hill. Fork right at the top to reach the bus terminus and car park at the northern end of Goodwick's Harbour Village.

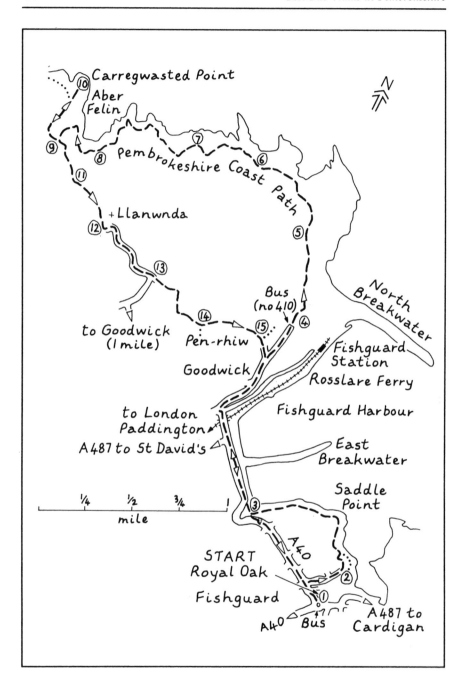

4. Go ahead along the Coast Path, keeping the sea on your right, with the harbour immediately below you. Dinas Head can be seen across Fishguard Bay. Begin with a fence on your left, then continue through bracken. Go ahead over a stile and along a wide path.

5. Do not be tempted by the walled path going left. Walk with a wall on your right towards the sea. Go left, as directed by a waymark post. Take a stile in the corner and pass Pen Anglas on your right. Bear right, keeping a wall on your left.

6. Continue across a stile in the corner and bear right, with a wall on your right. Go ahead over another three stiles and keep to the signposted Coast Path. After taking another stile, walk with a fence on your left and bear right through gorse.

7. Descend, cross a stile and walk with a fence on your left. Continue over two small footbridges,. then a third to cross a steam. Cross a subsequent stile and go right with the fenced path which turns left to climb beside a wall on your right. Go ahead to Aber Felin's bay.

8. Go ahead over a stile, follow the right-hand edge of a field, cross another stile and continue beside a fence on your left. Go inland to take a third stile and reach a signpost, which you will return to after visiting Carregwastad Point.

9. Descend to a footbridge. Cross it and climb the steep slope to a signpost. Bear right and cross a stile in the fence on your right to take the path to the memorial on Carregwastad Point.

10. Retrace your steps to the signpost at direction point 9. Bear right, then walk beside a fence on your left to a waymarked gate. Continue through it and across a field to the next gate.

11. A hedged track leads to another waymarked gate. Maintain your direction through a field, a gate, across a track and turn left to a stile. This gives access to Llanwnda. Pass St Gwyndaf's Church on your left.

12. Go ahead along the road and bear left at a fork, passing a cemetery on your right.

13. Go ahead at a crossing to follow a lane which passes a track on your right before bearing right and passing a house. Follow the lane as it turns left.

14. Continue through Pen-rhiw's farm-yard. Follow the concrete lane which is its access track.

15. Bear right above Goodwick to join the road at Harbour Village and retrace your steps back to Fishguard and the Royal Oak.

4. Dinas

Route: Dinas- Pwllgwaelod – Dinas Head – Cwm-yr-Eglwys -Dinas.

Distance: 4 miles. Moderate.

Map: OS Pathfinder 1010 (Cardigan & Dinas Head) and 1033 (Newport & Eglwyswrw).

Start: The Ship Aground, Dinas (SN 012389).

Access: Dinas is on the A487 between Fishguard and Newport. Bus no. 412 links Dinas with Haverfordwest, via Fishguard, and Cardigan, via Newport.

The Ship Aground, Dinas (03486 261)

Real ale and food are served in this authentic village pub, which dates from 1750. Opening hours are 11 am to 11 pm on weekdays, noon to 3 pm and 7 pm to 10.30 pm on Sundays.

The Sailors' Safety Inn

This remote pub does not seem to have a telephone number. It opens on a seasonal basis and sells ice-cream as well as the usual ale and snacks. Its name is a reminder that a light was shown here after dark to aid mariners in Fishguard Bay.

Dinas

Smuggling and wrecking must have been a way of life hereabouts before the 19th century.

Dinas Island sticks out almost like a stalwart resistance fighter surrounded by stormy seas. It rises to its highest point (466ft) at its head,
seemingly defying the waves, which seek to undermine it from within,
cutting a channel between Cwm-yr-Eglwys and Pwllgwaelod. This was,
indeed, a glacial melt-water channel. Hence the sense of Dinas Island,
although it is a peninsula. The redoubtable St Brynach recognised the
power of this place and both the ruined church in Cwm-yr-Eglwys and
the parish church on the road from Dinas Bryn-Henllan are dedicated to
this 5th century Irishman who became a Celtic saint. This part of Wales
was strongly influenced by the Irish during the 5th century and Brynach
appears to have married a local princess, with whom he had four
children. The saintly life then called him, perhaps as a result of commun-
ing with the angels on Carn Ingli (see the Newport Walk No. 5) and
there are tales of his dealing with an amorous woman, perhaps his wife,
who tried to lead him astray. His church in Cwm-yr-Eglwys suffered the
loss of all but its belfry and west wall in the great storm of 25th October,
1859. *The Royal Charter* and 113 other ships were wrecked off the coast of
Wales that night. Another storm in March, 1979, brought further damage
to the church and church-yard.

The coasting cargo vessel *Gramsbergen* sank off Dinas Island on 28th
November, 1954. She was sheltering in anticipation of her first bad storm
since being launched 6 months earlier. The anchor chain broke in a
heavy swell about 2 am and she hit the rocks before the engines could be
started. A Dutch seaman swam with a line to the cliffs (about 40 yards
away), where a local farmer helped him. The Fishguard lifeboat was
promptly on the scene to take off the Captain and the rest of the crew. A
rope fouled the lifeboat's propeller and she had to be towed to the
quay-side by the harbour launch (a former lifeboat). The 498 tons gross
ship sank in 6 fathoms of water.

On a fine day, look out for grey seals at Dinas Head, also for the
triangular dorsal fins of sea porpoises and for the sickle-shaped dorsal
fins and beak-like snouts of dolphins. You may also see gannets diving
for fish.

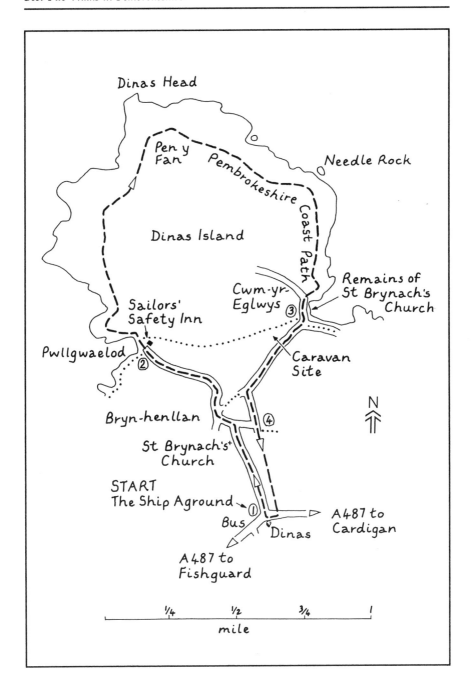

The Walk

1. Turn left, away from the A487 road. Pass St Brynach's Church on your left. Fork left to a T-junction at Bryn-henllan and turn right, as signposted for Pwllgwaelod. Ignore a No Through Road on your right. The road bears left and descends to the beach, old lime kilns and the Sailors' Safety Inn.

2. Turn right along the Coast Path, keeping the sea on your left. Walk around Dinas Head and eventually descend to Cwm-yr-Eglwys, where the ruined church is on your left.

3. Turn right along a lane and ignore a lane turning left. Go ahead to pass the entrance to the caravan site on your right. The lane's surface deteriorates as you climb. Bear left along what is once more a metalled lane and pass a house called Penllain on your right. Pass a road on your right and follow the metalled lane to its end.

4. Ignore the track going left. Take the signposted public footpath ahead. This muddy old green lane leads back to the A487 at Dinas. Turn right to return to The Ship Aground.

5. Newport

Route: Newport – Carn Ingli – Bedd Morris – Newport.

Distance: 6 miles. Strenuous.

Map: OS Pathfinder 1033 (Newport & Eglwyswrw).

Start: The Golden Lion, Newport (SN 059392).

Access: Newport is on the A487 between Cardigan and Fishguard. There is a good weekday bus service (no. 412) which runs between Haverfordwest and Cardigan via Fishguard and Newport.

The Golden Lion, Newport (0239 820321)

June Auckland from 'The Bill' has supped here, so sample the real ale and bar snacks, or eat in the restaurant. There is a beer garden, while bed and breakfast accommodation is available. Opening hours are 11 am to 11 pm on weekdays, noon to 3 pm and 7 pm to 10.30 pm on Sundays.

Newport

This 'new port' was established in 1191 by William Martin, whose grand-father had been the first Norman invader of this area. He had been driven out of the original Norman powerbase at Nevern by his father-in-law, Lord Rhys. The castle is seldom open to the public. St Mary's Church was founded by the Normans too, although a 6th century chapel, probably dedicated to St Curig, although St Brynach was also in these parts, may have stood near the estuary of the Afon Nyfer. St Brynach climbed Carn Ingli, whose name refers to the tradition that he is said to have communed with the angels on its 1138ft summit. Bedd Morris is an impressive standing stone.

The Walk

1. Go right, towards the centre of Newport. Turn left along Upper St
   Mary Street and bear right at is top to reach a junction. Turn left to
   pass the entrance to St Mary's Church on your left, pass Penffald on
   your right. The castle is above, on your right.

2. Fork right up a No Through Road. Bear left at its top junction and
   pass a cottage called Bryneithin on your left. Ignore a track going
   right as you continue to a junction of several tracks near cottages on
   your left. Turn right here along an uphill track.

Looking north from the 1138ft summit of Carn Ingli

3. Go ahead through a gate and walk straight up the common to the
   jagged 1138ft peak of Carn Ingli, on the skyline. The final ascent
   entails an undignified scramble over the rocks.

4. Descend to the moorland on the far side of the summit and aim

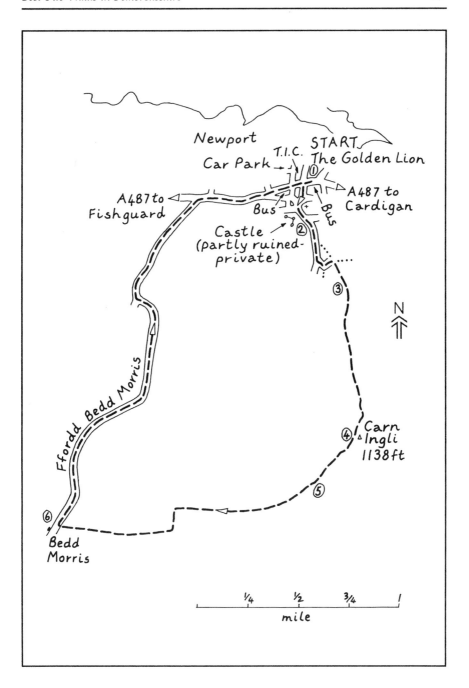

towards a fence on your right ahead.

5. Bear right with the fence for nearly one mile, then turn left, then right
   with the fence for another half mile. When the fence turns left again,
   go straight ahead to reach a road at the standing stone known as
   Bedd Morris.

6. Turn right down the road (Ffordd Bedd Morris) back to the A487.
   Turn right to return to Newport and follow the main road through
   the town (named successively West Street, Bridge Street and East
   Street) back to the Golden Lion, on your left.

6. Trefin

Route: Trefin – Coast Path – Porth-gain – Henllys -Old Mill -Trwyn Llwyd – Trefin.

Distance: 5 miles. Moderate.

Map: OS Pathfinder 1032 (Fishguard).

Start: The Ship Inn, Trefin (SM 838325).

Access: Trefin is just over one mile north of the A487 road near Square and Compass, between Fishguard and St David's. There is a weekday bus service (no. 411) linking Trefin with St David's and Fishguard.

The Ship Inn, Trefin (0348 831445)

Apart from the years between 1972 and 1988, this pub has been kept within the same family since the 18th century.

There's Welsh singing most evenings, while live music is a feature of Saturday nights. Real ale is served, while the food includes a children's menu and a vegetarian choice. There is a beer garden, while both bed and breakfast accommodation and self-catering accommodation are available. Admire a painting done by a survivor of the *Ragna*, which was wrecked near here. The ship's anchor also adorns the pub. Opening hours are noon to 3 pm and 6 pm to 11 pm on weekdays, noon to 3 pm and 7 pm to 10.30 pm on Sundays.

The Sloop Inn, Porth-gain (0348 831449)

If sea conditions are favourable, fresh local crab sandwiches and salads (with generous helpings and fillings) are available. There's real ale and other food, of course, while summer Sundays see the pub open all afternoon to sell ice-cream and other non-alcoholic refreshments. You'll meet other walkers here as it's on the Coast Path. Actors and TV stars such as Jerome Flyn have been known to drop by. Local memorabilia of

the industrial port are on display. Opening hours are 11.30 am to 11 pm
on weekdays, noon to 3 pm and 7 pm to 10.30 pm on Sundays.

The Sloop Inn

Trefin

Pronounced Tre-veen (and not Trevine, although this is the English
version of this place-name), this village is founded on solid rock, dating
from the Ordovician era 500 million years ago. Pre-historic monuments
stand nearby, while one of the early Bishops of St David's had his (now
lost) palace here. The youth hostel makes it a staging post for Coastal
Path walkers. Their route takes them past the ruins of a mill. When it fell
into disuse in 1918; its fate inspired the Archdruid Crwys to pen the
following lines:

'Nid yw'r felin heno'n malu
Yn Nhrefin ym min y môr,
Trodd y merlin olaf adre
Dan ei bwn o drothwy's ddôr'.

(The old mill isn't turning tonight in
Trefin by the side of the sea,
The donkey doesn't carry his heavy
load there anymore).

Ruins of the old mill

Porth-gain

The harbour saw the export of bricks, slates and road-stones between 1837 and 1931. The remains of great bins used to hold crushed stone and one of the old brickworks can be seen, while on either side of the harbour entrance are navigation marks.

A little bit of the Industrial Revolution has intruded on the rugged natural splendour of this coastline. In the summer of 1909, 13000 tons of crushed stone was exported in 101 shipments (there was a special fleet of six 350-ton coasters) in order to facilitate the programme of metalling the nation's roads.

The Walk

1. Go left and pass the weaving centre, craft shop and tea-rooms on your left, then a holy well near the roadside on your left. Descend with the road to a Coast Path signpost above the ruins of the old mill but do not take this path yet. It will form the final section of this route. Meanwhile go ahead with the road.

2. Turn right with the signposted Coast Path over a stone step stile at Swyn-y-Don. Bear right to cross a second, wooden, step stile and go left with the Coast Path. Keep the sea on your right as you pass the farmhouse on your left, then walk beside a fence. Continue over a series of stiles. Follow the waymarked and well-trodden path to Porth-gain, with its old industrial harbour.

3. Leave the Coast Path by turning left, inland. Ignore a track forking left. Go ahead to pass the Sloop Inn on your left. Continue along the lower road to pass the telephone box on your right. When the road bears right, fork left along the signposted public footpath (a firm track).

4. At the next signpost, turn right to cross a footbridge and bear left over a waymarked stile. Go ahead through a gap and along the left-hand edge of a field. Continue through a kissing-gate and follow the hedge on your left to another kissing-gate in the next corner. Go

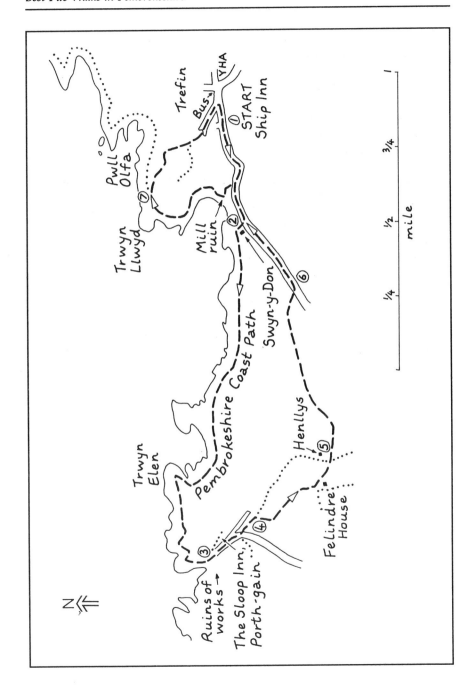

through it, across a paddock and over a stile beside a gate. Turn left along a track, passing Felindre House on your right.

5. Follow the track past Henllys farm on your left. Maintain your direction when the track ends, going ahead through a gate and walking along the right-hand edge of the field to a gate in the next corner. Bear very slightly right across the next field to a stile in the corner ahead. Cross it to reach a road.

6. Turn left along the road, back towards Trefin. When you reach the first Coast Path signpost encountered as you left Trefin, turn left off the road. Divert left to visit the ruins of the old mill. As you stand above the mill, bear right to follow the Coast Path over a footbridge. Keep the sea on your left as you take the Coast Path to a signposted path junction at the top of a cliff on Trwyn Llwyd.

7. Cross the stile beside the signpost and turn right, along the inland path. Soon bear left with this to walk with a fence on your right. Continue along a fenced, grassy, track, which gains a firmer surface and a wall on your right as it approaches Trefin. Join an estate road and follow it down to the centre of the village. The bus shelter and the youth hostel are on your left. Turn right to return to the Ship Inn.

7. Casmael (Puncheston)

Route: Casmael (Puncheston) — Ffordd Mynydd — Llygad-yr-haul — Parsonage — Castlebythe — Casmeal (Puncheston).

Distance: 4$\frac{1}{2}$ miles. Moderate.

Maps: OS Pathfinder 1033 (Newport & Eglwyswrw) and 1057 (Ambleston and Llandissilio).

Start: The Drovers' Arms, Casmeal (Puncheston) (SN 007297)

Access: Casmael (Puncheston) is reached by minor roads and is three miles west of the B4329 (Haverfordwest-Eglwyswrw road) at Henry's Moat. The no. 343 bus runs here on Fridays only from Fishguard. Oh, for the days of steam trains!

The Drovers' Arms, Casmael (Puncheston) (0348 881469)

Drovers used this inn for centuries until the railway made them redundant. The pub suffered a fire in 1957 and has been partly rebuilt. There is a ghost of a little child who is said to have died here long ago. Real ale and food are served. Opening hours are 11 am to 11 pm on weekdays, noon to 3 pm and 7 pm to 10.30 pm on Sundays.

Casmael (Puncheston)

Railway engineers must have romance in their souls to extend the iron way to places like Puncheston – either that or delusions of grandeur. There had already been a line from Clynderwen (on the surviving railway to Fishguard, at a point just west of Whitland) to the quarries at Rosebush (see Walk 13 for details) when the Great Western Railway opened its line between Clynderwen and Letterston junction in 1895. The Great Western Railway had bought it to forestall its builders, the North Pembroke and Fishguard Railway, from offering it as an alternative route to the new harbour at Fishguard to their competitors the London and North Western Railway.

When the Great Western Railway opened a new line from Clarbeston Road (the junction for the surviving Fishguard and Milford Haven lines) to Letterston junction (to join the tracks on to Fishguard) in 1906, this line heard its death knell. Apart from the steep gradient, there was a tunnel with a bend in it that couldn't be negotiated by powerful locomotives pulling boat trains. Closed in 1917, the track was actually lifted and sent to France, only to fail to arrive because of enemy action. The line from Clynderwen to Puncheston re-opened in 1921 and the Puncheston-Letterston junction section followed suit in 1923. it was a forlorn gesture as the whole line was to close in 1937 and the Letterston-Puncheston section was to never re-open. The tracks further east around Maenclochog were used for target practice by the RAF and the USAF in the second world war. Goods traffic did return to the route from Clynderwen to Puncheston in 1945, however, until final closure in 1949.

The Drovers' Arms

The Walk

1. Go right, ignore a road on your right and walk past the sewage works on your right. Bear right at a fork, as signposted for Maenclochog.

2. After about 100 yards, bear left along a gravel track with high hedged banks. Look out for badger setts on your right.

3. Fork right along an enclosed grassy track. When this emerges in the corner of a field, do not continue along it but do turn right down the right-hand side of the field. This track leads to the farm house and buildings of Llygad-yr-haul ('the eye of the sun').

4. Take the farm access track which turns right. Pass another farm house on your left, then turn left and follow the track as it bears right across open land towards Windy Hill Farm.

5. Turn left down a track which continues through a gateway on your right and down the left-hand side of the next field to the road as a private, firm, track. The public bridleway does not take the gateway into the field on your right. It can be very muddy in wet weather as it bears left to a gate in the bottom neck of this field and continues as an enclosed path beside a stream to reach the road near its parallel, firm but private, neighbouring track.

6. Go right along the road for 50 yards, then fork left down a track signposted as a No Through Road. This crosses the course of a dismantled railway and continues over a footbridge across a stream, near a cataract. Bear right to pass a disused quarry on your left.

7. Ignore the track going to a farm on your right. Continue beside a fence on your right along a firm track at the foot of a slope on your left bearing trees and gorse bushes. When the firm track turns sharply left uphill, leave it and go straight ahead through a gate and along the left-hand edge of a field. Continue along the side of the next field, past Parsonage Farm on your left and along its access lane to a road.

8. Turn right along the road. Turn right at Castlebythe, as signposted
for Puncheston (1 mile). Go left in the village to return to the Drovers'
Arms.

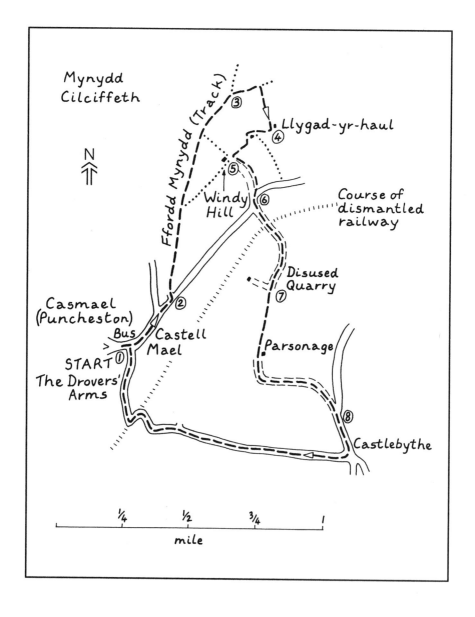

8. Crymych

Route: Crymych — Foeldrygarn — Golden Road — Carn Menyn - Beddarthur — Cerrig Meibion Arthur — Mynachlog-ddu — Crymych

Distance: 12 miles. Strenuous.

Map: OS Pathfinder 1033 (Newport & Eglwyswrw).

Start: The Crymych Arms, Crymych (SN 183340).

Access: Crymych is on the A478 about 10 miles south of Cardigan, from where the no. 430 bus runs an infrequent weekday service. The bus stops near the pub, at the northern end of the village.

The Crymych Arms, Crymych (0239 831435)

There are rumours of a ghost having haunted this old pub, but it hasn't appeared lately. Perhaps you'll be the chosen one should you stay here for bed and breakfast. Real ale and food are served. Opening hours are 11 am to 3.30 pm and 5.30 pm to 11 pm from Mondays to Thursdays, 11 am to 11 pm on Fridays and Saturdays, then noon to 3 pm and 7 pm to 10.30 pm on Sundays. This is an old drovers inn.

The Magical Preselis

Step into an enchanted world inhabited by the ghosts of pre-history on these broad, bare, windswept hills. Until the Romans came, there must have been a fairly dense population here, surrounded by trees. Now there are only the rectangular acres of conifer plantation. Climb Foeldrygarn for the view and much more. Pick out the Black Mountain to the east, Snowdonia to the north and, even, the Wicklow Hills over the Irish Sea in the west. The hill is named after three Bronze Age cairns at its summit. No doubt these are connected by leys or spirit paths with the surrounding peaks, such as Carn Ingli. So special is the volcanic ash up here that five stones found at Stonehenge have been identified as coming from here. Perhaps they were carried along the Golden Road, the nearby track which earned its name when gold from the Wicklow Hills was carried along it in the Bronze Age. Welsh Black Cattle were driven along it in the 19th century, when Crymych was an assembly point for the drovers to begin the journey to market in England.

Nearly all of Stonehenge's blue-stones came from Carn Menyn. Similar stones still litter the site. They were formed when frost shattered the bed-rock during the last Ice Age. Altogether 60 of these spotted dolerite can be seen at Stonehenge, as the inner circle and the inner horseshoe. The legend that they came from Ireland is a reminder that this part of Wales did count as Irish in the time of Merlin. King Arthur rode this way to fight the Twrch Trwyth (stinking boar) and one of his many graves is Beddarthur, where 15 stones from an oval. All the details of Arthur's campaign are in the story of *Culhwch and Olwen* in *The Mabinogion*. Arthur had pursued the Twrch Trwyth from Ireland and caught up with the enemy here. Standing at bay in Cwm Cerwyn Twrch Trwyth slew four of Arthur's champions, then four more including Arthur's son Gwydre. Presumably a second of Arthur's sons was killed because there is a monument below Foel Cwmcerwyn in the form of two standing stones. These are the Cerrig Meibion Arthur. If Arthur had had an heir the later Battle of Camlan need not have been fought and Britain might still be a Welsh-speaking nation.

The Walk

1. Go down the main road in Crymych, passing the fire station and schools on your left. Take the first turning on your right after the schools and follow this road to a T-junction, where you go left. Bear right along a fenced track.

2. Reach a junction with a second track coming from your left and go ahead over a stile. Immediately bear right along a path to the summit of Foeldrygarn. Bear left when descending to return to the old green road known as the Golden Road and go right along it to pass a conifer plantation on your left. Divert left to visit the rócky outcrops of Carn Menyn, then return to the old road.

3. Head west along the Golden Road to find Beddarthur just below the brow of a hill ahead. Continue to descend to a pass where a distinct moorland path comes in from your right.

4. Turn left to follow an old track above the boggy valley on your right. Bear left with it towards a road. As you approach the road, turn sharply right along another grassy track to reach Cerrig Meibion Arthur.

5. Retrace your steps to the path junction and continue to the road.

6. Go left along the road and keep left when it forks.

7. Bear left at the road junction at Mynachlog-ddu and follow the road back to the T-junction where you turn right to retrace your steps into Crymych.

The path ascending Foeldygarn

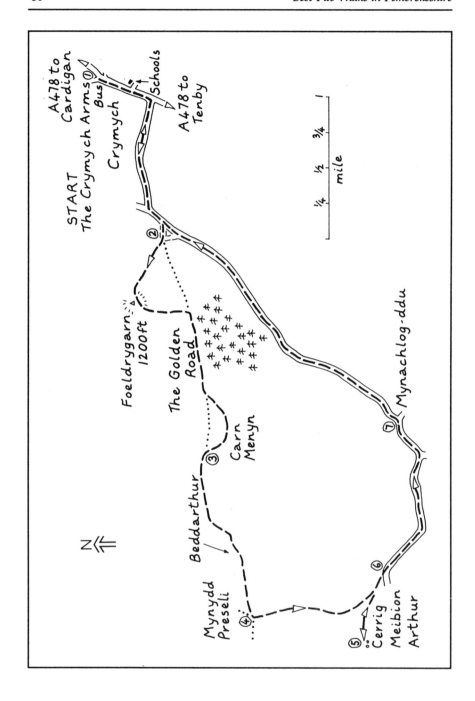

9. St David's

Route: St David's — St Justinian's — Pembrokeshire Coast Path — Whitesands Bay — St David's.

Distance: 6 miles. Easy.

Map: OS Pathfinder 1055 (St David's & Ramsey Island).

Start: The Farmers' Arms, St David's (SM 752253).

Access: St David's can be reached along the A487 from Fishguard or Haverfordwest. Both of these towns have railway stations and buses numbers 340 from Haverfordwest and 411 from Fishguard run on weekdays.

The Farmers' Arms, St David's (0437 720328)

This pub is about 150 years old and was previously a pair of cottages. Real ale and food are served, while there is a beer garden on the cathedral side. Customers claim to have seen the ghost of a woman walking across the Coxswain's Bar, which is decorated with lifeboat memorabilia. Opening hours are 11 am to 11 pm on weekdays, noon to 3 pm and 7 pm to 10.30 pm on Sundays.

St David's

The cathedral occupies a site where Christ has been worshipped since the sixth century, making it senior to Canterbury. Pilgrims have come here for centuries and three pilgrimages to St David's were reckoned to equal one to Jerusalem. The cathedral isn't seen until you arrive on the ridge overlooking its hollow, however. This is a reminder that secrecy was important in the days when Irish, and then Viking, pirates raided inland from the nearby coast. The first building here was burned down in 645, while Vikings sacked the cathedral in 1078, killing Bishop Abraham.

St David's Cathedral

St David is the Patron Saint of Wales and his Saint's Day is on 1st March, the anniversary of his death in the late 580s. Born nearby at St Non's in 500 or a few years before, the young David travelled widely before returning to his homeland. He is known to have been at Glastonbury, while legend states that he went to Jerusalem, where the Patriarch appointed him as an Archbishop. The journey is found in the lives of Saints Teilo and Padarn also, with these two saints being consecrated as Bishops by the Patriarch. David brought an altar back from Jerusalem which resides in his cathedral. Back at the place which now bears his name, David founded a religious community which seems to have been vegan. Not only were bread and herbs preferred to flesh but the only drink was water, while David drew the plough with a yoke on his shoulders, rather than enslaving oxen. Property was owned in common and much time was devoted to prayer. Conversation was limited to what was necessary. Warned, it is said, by an angel of his death a week in advance, St David asked his followers to remember him by the little things he did. His bones are kept in a chest behind the altar.

William the Conqueror noticed the pre-eminence of St David's and came here in 1081 to pray and impress the Welsh with a show of Norman force. The Normans arranged for one of their own to become Bishop (Rome never recognised the Archbishopric) in 1115. This led to the erection of the present building. Bishop Gower built the Palace in the 14th century. This suffered from neglect after the Reformation and is now in the care of Cadw (Heritage in Wales). The Dissolution caused the transfer of the tomb of Edmund Tudor, father of Henry VII, from Carmarthen to here. This tomb now stands before the High Altar. When the church in Wales was disestablished in 1920 the new Archbishop of Wales entertained the Patriarchs of Jerusalem, Alexandria and Byzantium, thus honouring the ancient link between the Celtic and Eastern Churches.

St Justinian's

St Justinian was a friend of St David whose bones are now in the same chest as St David's behind the altar in the cathedral. Murdered on Ramsey Island, he was initially buried at the old chapel here. Take a boat trip around Ramsey Island from the lifeboat station during the tourist season. This lifeboat station was built in 1911/12, before the sinking of the cargo steamship *Count D'Aspremont* in Ramsey Sound on 9th December, 1903. The crew were saved in their own boat.

Whitesands Bay

There is a prehistoric forest under the attractive sands of this beach. The Roman station of Menapia (Menevia) marked the end of the prehistoric Golden Road and the ancient departure point for Ireland. St Patrick is said to have set sail for the Emerald Isle from here.

The Walk

1. Go right down Goat Street. Ignore the signposted lane to St Non's Chapel on your left and fork right downhill. Pass the Bishop's Palace on your right, go ahead across the River Alun and pass a car park on your left.

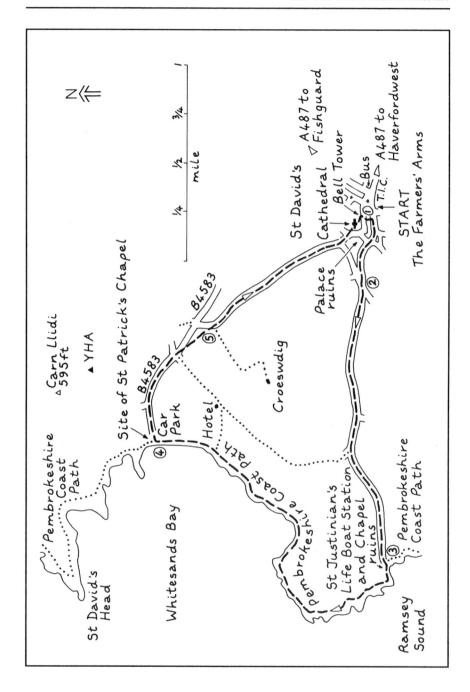

2. Bear left at a road junction, as signposted for St Justinian. Soon fork right and continue past a road on your left. Bear left at the next fork and continue to the end of the road overlooking St Justinian's lifeboat station and with the ruined chapel on your right.

3. Turn right along the cliff-top Coast Path, with the sea and Ramsey Island on your left. Pass above the beach at Whitesand Bay.

4. Turn right, inland, through the car park and along the B4583 road. Pass an access lane to Whitesand Bay Hotel on your right and go ahead beside a power or telephone line which diverges from the road on your left.

5. Go ahead along a lane, passing an access track to Croeswdig on your right. After one mile, when the lane bends to the right, go straight ahead down a track to pass the ruins of the Bishop's Palace on your right. Take the old stone footbridge over the River Alun to go ahead to St David's Cathedral. From its main entrance (South Porch), bear left up to an old fortified gateway (the Bell Tower), pass through it and immediately turn right along a lane. Emerge at the side of the Farmers' Arms on your left.

The Farmers' Arms

10. Solva

Route: Lower Solva — Pembrokeshire Coast Path — Burial Chamber — Lower Solva.

Distance: 3 miles. Moderate.

Map: OS Pathfinder 1055 (St David's & Ramsey Island) or 1056 (Newgale & Wolf's Castle).

Start: The Ship Inn, Solva (SM 806244).

Access: Solva is on the A487 between Haverfordwest and St David's. Bus no. 340 runs between these two places on weekdays.

The Ship Inn, Solva (0437 721247)

This 17th century pub has a resident ghost, a former licensee known as 'Ma' Raggett. The daughter of an earlier landlord married Henry Whiteside, the designer of the lighthouse on The Smalls (ocean rocks well to the south-west of here), built in 1776. This lighthouse became the most profitable in the world, collecting dues from passing ships. The real ale is also well worth a mention. The choice includes Solva's own real ale, brewed in the village. There is an inviting open fire in winter, while summer days can be enjoyed in the beer garden overlooking the river. Food is also served. Bar opening hours are 11 am to 11 pm on weekdays, noon to 3 pm and 7 pm to 10.30 pm on Sundays.

Solva

This village has a picturesque harbour, which is a drowned valley or ria. The first small lighthouse was built here and taken 22 miles out to sea for erection on the tiny rocks. Coastal trade made this a busy little harbour in the late 18th century, as witnessed by the surviving lime kilns. There is evidence of an ancient settlement on the headland on the eastern side of the harbour, although the burial chamber near St Elvis Farm, has collapsed.

Smuggling and wrecking (by showing lights to attract ships onto the rocks) were common here, indeed vital to the local economy in the 18th century. No doubt St Elvis would not have approved. He was the Saint who brought up David in the sure knowledge that the boy would become a famous saint.

The Walk

1. Go left along the pavement of the A487 and fork left into the car park. Cross a footbridge in the left-hand corner to go over the River Solva and bear slightly left to reach steps. Bear right up these to follow the narrow Coast Path.

2. Climb to a fork and bear right down to a row of old lime kilns. Continue through a small wooden gate to ascend with the Coast Path above Solva Harbour on your right.

3. Bear left with the Coast Path. Descend to a footbridge crossing the stream in the next valley. Go past a pebble beach on your right and continue along the Coast Path above the sea on your right.

4. Bear left at a Coast Path signpost, keeping above the sea on your right. Go ahead over stiles in two fences and cross a third stile in a fence just before the peninsula of Pen Dinas.

5. Turn left, as signposted, to follow the public footpath inland, walking with a fence on your left. Take a gap into the next field, walk with a hedge on your left and continue over a stile beside a gate in the corner ahead. Follow a broad, enclosed, track towards St Elvis Farm.

The view out to sea and Black Rock from direction point 4

6. Cross a stile to the right of a gate and immediately turn left through a small wooden gate to take a track leading from the farm, now away to your right. Ignore a waymarked stile on your right as the enclosed track bears left to a gate with a stile beside it.

7. Continue over the stile beside the gate to walk with a fence on your left and above the valley on your right. Bear left with the track and descend towards the sea. Turn right over the footbridge to retrace your steps along the Coast Path, with the harbour on your left, to Solva and the Ship Inn.

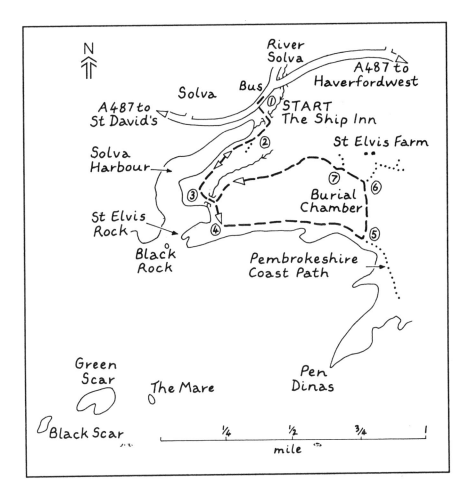

11. Nolton Haven

Route: Nolton Haven – Pembrokeshire Coast Path – Druidston Haven – Welsh Way – Nolton Haven – Pembrokeshire Coast Path – Disused Colliery – Welsh Way – Nolton Haven.

Distance: 4 miles. Moderate.

Map: OS Pathfinder 1079 (Haverfordwest).

Start: The Mariners' Inn, Nolton Haven. (SM 806244).

Access: Nolton Haven is on the coast and can be approached along a minor road from the A487 at Roch some two miles to the north-east. Roch is served by bus no. 340 on weekdays from St David's and Haverfordwest (the nearest railway station).

The Mariners' Inn, Nolton Haven (0437 710469)

Sea-faring memorabilia decorate the walls and ceiling of this pub, which dates from 1749, when this cove was used by smugglers.

Real ale and bar snacks are available, while there is a restaurant and bed and breakfast accommodation. 'Norman' the ghost has the disconcerting habit of smashing lightbulbs. Bar opening hours are 11 am to 11 pm on weekdays, noon to 3 pm and 7 pm to 10.30 pm on Sundays.

Nolton Haven

Coal from the nearby colliery used to be exported from here. The coal was stored on an embankment at the northern corner of the beach. The old colliery near Trefrane at the northern end of the walk opened in 1850 and closed in 1905, although there were plans to re-open it in 1915. A chimney survives. At the southern end, Druidston does not refer to a druid, but to Drue, a Norman knight.

Rickets Head is well-named as it is crumbling away. The Welsh Way was the ancient track used by pilgrims going between St Ishmael's and St David's (and thus avoiding a dangerous coastal voyage).

The Coast Path, north of Nolton Haven

The Walk

1. Go left up the road to a fork, where you turn right along the signposted Coast Path. This goes above the United Reformed Church before bearing left along the cliff-top above the beach on your right. Follow the Coast Path for one mile, almost to Druidston Haven. You eventually go down steps to a small valley, where you leave the Coast Path.

2. Turn left inland up the valley path above a stream on your right.

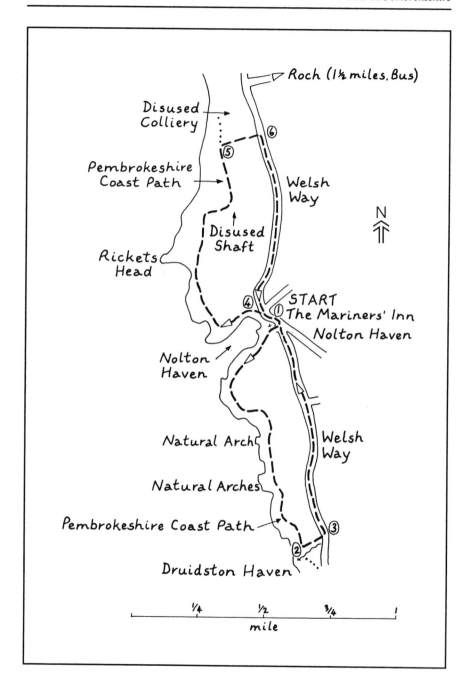

3. Turn left along a metalled lane back to Nolton Haven. Go left at the road junction by the church and pass the pub on your right. When level with the telephone box on your right, bear left along the signposted Coast Path past the beach on your left.

4. Climb steps to a signpost and bear left across a stile to follow the Coast Path above the bay on your left. Bear right to walk with the open sea on your left.

5. When the fence on your right turns right, go inland beside it, past a disused colliery on your left. Pass a pond on your left then go ahead over a stile beside a gate to reach a metalled lane.

6. Turn right along the lane back to Nolton Haven and the Mariners' Inn.

12. Wolf's Castle

Route: Wolf's Castle – Treffgarne Farm – Nolton – Treffgarne Gorge – Treffgarne Farm – Wolf's Castle.

Distance: 6 miles. Moderate.

Map: OS Pathfinder 1056 (Newgale & Wolf's Castle).

Start: Wolfe Inn, Wolf's Castle (SM 957262).

Access: Wolf's Castle is on the A40 between Fishguard and Haverford-west. Bus no. 412 stops here on its way between Cardigan and Haverfordwest via Fishguard. This is a good weekday service.

Wolfe Inn, Wolf's Castle (0348 87662)

The name has nothing to do with wolves or General Wolfe. A Viking named Ulf came this way and built the castle. This pub is old but has

only been called the Wolfe Inn since 1964. It used to be called The Commercial before being closed by the Temperance Movement and serving as a sober post office and shop between 1918 and 1964. It has a cosy fire, real ale, food (including a vegetarian choice) and offers bed and breakfast accommodation. Opening hours are 11 am to 3 pm and 6.30 pm to 11 pm on weekdays, noon to 3 pm and 7 pm to 10.30 pm on Sundays.

Treffgarne Gorge

This delightful wooded slope hides the railway line to Fishguard Harbour. Otters and salmon frequent the Western Cleddau river. The two trains a day hardly disturb their peace but the railway very nearly didn't come here at all. It had to come, however, to fulfil a prophecy made in the 18th century. Sarah, the wife of Thomas Evans of Penfeidr Farm, near Great Treffgarne Mountain at grid reference SM 946236, was renowned for her visions of the future. One day she described a remarkable sight of a number of wagons joined together and going very fast one after another. There were no horses to pull them, but the leading wagon appeared to be on fire as she clearly saw smoke coming from it. Over 50 years later Isambard Kingdom Brunel started to construct a railway in this gorge (originally on the same side of the river as this walk) but work on it ceased in 1851 because of the potato famine in Ireland. Brunel took his line to Milford Haven instead. Later a railway was constructed to Fishguard, but running well north of the present route. The prophecy seemed to be false, but the Great Western Railway found they had to lay tracks here in the end as the other line proved unsuitable for a fast direct service between London and the port of Fishguard. The visions of both Brunel and Mrs Evans were fulfilled.

The Walk

1. With your back to the pub, ignore the road going sharply left, but do go left along the pavement of the A40. Cross a bridge over the railway then fork left past the village shop on your left to take the older bridge across the river and turn right to follow the road under the A40. Go ahead over a bridge across a tributary river and bear right at a fork. Soon pass Upper Danbarch, then the access track down to Lletty-llwydrew. Turn right when you reach a T-junction.

2. When Treffgarne Farm is on your right, turn left to follow a concrete lane which leads away from it and is waymarked with a yellow arrow on a post. Pass an access track to Croft on your left. Pass under power lines, and after one hundred yards, turn right over a cattle grid, as signposted. Follow a track across a field, parallel to a hedge on your right. Continue as waymarked beside the hedge on your right in the next field.

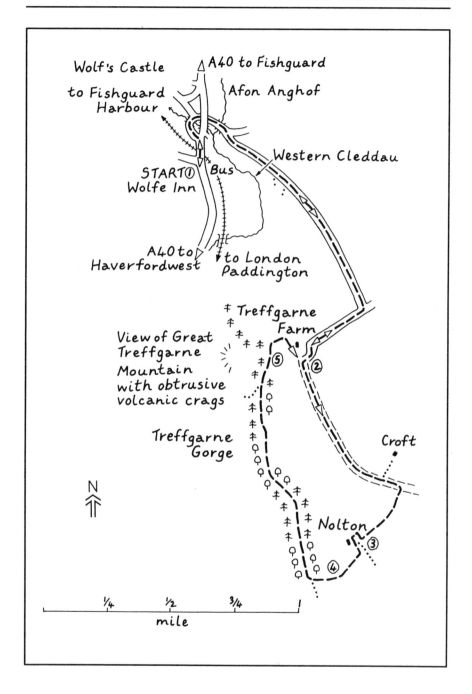

3. Turn right through a gate at the bottom of the field and follow the waymarked track past Nolton. Ignore a track leading away from the farm-house but do take the field-gate to the right of it to follow the path waymarked with yellow arrows. This starts along the left-hand side of the field before turning right to cross the centre of the field. Go through a waymarked gate in the wall ahead.

4. Bear right to pass an old farm building on your right, then a big white house on your left. Follow a woodland path to a waymarked junction and turn right. Pass from broad-leaved woodland to a plantation of conifers by crossing a stile ahead. Walk with the perimeter fence on your right, then cross a steam and descend with the waymarked path to a junction. Turn right uphill. Come to a waymark post and bear left as directed by the yellow arrow. Reach the upper perimeter fence and turn left to walk with it on your right.

5. Go ahead over a stile in the corner. Keeping the fence on your right, go ahead over two streams, reach a waymark post and bear right. Turn right through the yard of Treffgarne Farm. Pass the farm-house on your left before turning left to rejoin the access road. Go left to retrace your steps to Wolf's Castle, remembering to turn left at the next junction.

13. Rosebush

Route: Rosebush – Pantmaenog Forest – Golden Road – Rosebush.

Distance: 5 miles. Strenuous.

Map: OS Pathfinder 1033 (Newport & Eglwyswrw) and 1057 (Ambleston & Llandissilio).

Start: Tafarn Sinc Preseli (SN 076295).

Access: Rosebush used to have a railway. Now it is reduced to a bus on workdays only from Fishguard. Operated by Richards Brothers (0239 820751), this doesn't allow for day-trips from Fishguard to Rosebush but it does make it possible to reach this blessed spot by bus (no. 421) and stay here for at least a couple of nights (at the Old Post Office, tel. 0437 532205). Motorists have it easier, with Rosebush just off the B4313 between Narberth and Fishguard.

Tafarn Sinc Preseli (0437 532214)

Formerly the Precelly Hotel, this monument to Victorian confidence (and vision?), is clad in corrugated metal. Rather than close the railway when it was no longer needed to carry slate or boat passengers from Fishguard, an attempt was made to turn Rosebush into a spa and to attract health-seeking tourists to it. They were squeezed into tiny rooms but you can't emulate them as bed and breakfast is no longer available. Real ale is and the children's playground near the beer garden where the old railway ran is very popular in the summer. Opening hours are noon to 11 pm on weekdays, noon to 3 pm and 7 pm to 10.30 pm on Sundays. In the winter the pub only opens after 5 pm.

The Old Post Office (0437 532205)

This isn't a pub but it does remain open all day throughout the year as a licensed restaurant, bistro and tea-rooms. Bed and breakfast accommodation is available and ramblers are especially welcome. This former quarry-manager's house was the hamlet's shop and Post Office before adopting its present role in 1979. Stay here and explore the famous Golden Road!

The bar in the Old Post Office

Rosebush

The slate quarries made this place. Dark blue in colour, they were used widely for roofing purposes. The Narberth Road and Maenclochog Railway was constructed to export them. Its presence encouraged the development of this wilderness for tourists. Amazingly, the Great Western Railway even re-laid the track after it had been lifted during the First World War. This new track was finally taken up in 1952, three years after the last (goods) train ran on it. It is possible to understand why the Great Western Railway gambled on Rosebush, however. It is a fascinating spot in the magical Preselis. Stay here a few days to explore. The old slate quarries now form artificial lakes. Industrial archaeology can appear very beautiful here. Above all this are firm forest tracks through à forest of exotic conifers. At the very top, on the windswept plateau, is the prehistoric Golden Road. If the day is fine, divert to climb the 1760ft summit of Foel Cwmcerwyn on your return leg and enjoy a marvellous view.

The Walk

1. Go left from the tavern and turn left along the lane. This is signposted as a No Through Road and passes the Old Post Office (tea-room, bistro, licensed restaurant with bed and breakfast accommodation) and a telephone box on your left. Follow the private road but public bridleway past disused quarries on your right.

2. Go ahead through a gate into the forest. Ignore a track going left, continue with the firm track ahead for 250 yards before forking left from it along the bridleway at the foot of the forest.

3. Rejoin the firm track coming through the forest from your right and go ahead with it. Bear left at two successive forks as you climb to the top of the forest.

4. Emerge from the forest through a gate and turn right along the prehistoric Golden Road (see Walk 8 Crymych), keeping the forest and its perimeter fence on your right. When the fence turns right, follow it to cross a stile in the next corner and continue with the forest fence on your right.

5. Go ahead though a gate and keep beside the forest fence on your right. Cut across the mouth of a recess in this fence. Go ahead through another gate with a fence now on your left. Continue along a firm, fenced, track downhill, leaving the forest behind on your right.

6. Turn right over a waymarked stile and cross a field, passing a row of trees on your left, to cross another stile ahead. Bear left, as waymarked, to take an opening onto a track which soon bears right downhill to a farm. Continue down its access lane to the road at Rosebush. Go right for 50 yards to return to the tavern, on your left.

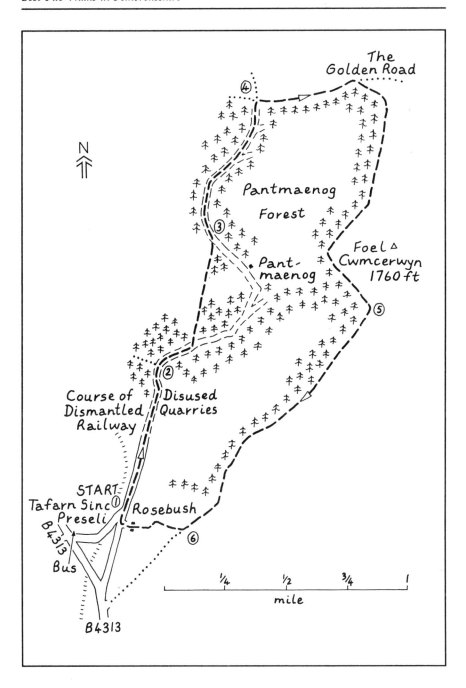

14. Llanddewi Velfrey

Route: Parc-y-lan Inn – St David's Church – White Mill – Caerau Gaer – Parc-y-lan Inn.

Distance: 3 miles. Moderate.

Map: OS Pathfinder 1080 (Narberth).

Start: Parc-y-lan Inn, Llanddewi Velfrey (SN 147169).

Access: Parc-y-lan stands beside the A40 road at Llanddewi Velfrey, between Narberth and Whitland. Buses numbers 322 and 323 connect Llanddewi Velfrey with Haverfordwest and Carmarthen.

Parc-y-lan Inn (0834 860532)

This pubs name means 'Top of the Meadow'. It stands beside the old turnpike road between London and the port of Fishguard. The original pub, which existed in the 19th century, was housed in what is now the restaurant part of the building. Real ale and bar snacks are served, while bed and breakfast accommodation is available. Opening hours are 11 am to 11 pm on weekdays, noon to 3 pm and 7 pm to 10.30 pm on Sundays.

Llanddewi Velfrey

St David's Church accounts for the first part of this place name. The Normans rendered the Welsh name for the commote of Efelffre into Velfrey. This is an ancient settlement, with two Iron Age enclosures located to the north of the 6th century church. Bronze Age sites dating back to 2500 BC have also been identified. The prehistoric ridgeway probably ran along the minor road followed from direction point 6 to point 7.

The line of the modern A40 road is a new one and the cluster of buildings beside it, including the pub at the start of this walk were once known as 'Commercial'. An old forge once existed next to Parc-y-lan Inn.

Walking south of Llanddewi Velfrey

St David's Church's new rector in 1851 was Richard Lewis. He went on to become a distinguished Bishop of Llandaff (Cardiff), but not before being initially rejected for this parish by the Bishop of St David's becuase he didn't speak the Welsh language. It took an appeal to the Archbishop of Canterbury and two attempts at a Welsh examination before he was finally accepted. He was buried here in 1905.

Look out for buzzards and kestrels on this walk, while there may by herons near White Mill. Spring sees the woodland carpeted with blue-bells.

The Walk

1. Go left to pass the war memorial and the road to Llanfallteg on your left. Turn right to cross the A40 carefully to the bus shelter and go left to continue your previous direction along the pavement. Soon bear right down a minor road.

2. Go ahead at a junction with another road to take the track which goes through gateposts and is signposted as a bridleway. This begins with a fence on your left and woodland on your right, then bears right through the woodland. Continue with trees on your left and a fence on your right. Pass the access track to the ruins of Plas-crwn on your left.

3. Pass the track to Cwmllefrith on your left. Bear right to descend with a fine view across the Lampeter Vale on your left. Pass Cwmllan farm and follow the track around a bend in the wooded hollow. Ignore the track descending to the Old Vicarage on your left.

4. Reach a signposted cross-paths. Divert left to visit St David's Church before resuming your previous direction, soon passing houses on your left. Turn left to descend with the tree-lined track, whose surface may be muddy in wet weather, to reach a metalled lane.

5. Turn right up the lane, soon passing the access track to White Mill on your left.

6. Turn right at a T-junction to follow a road.

7. Turn left over a metal bar stile to follow a signposted public footpath downhill. Near the foot of the pasture, descend with a hedge on your right to take a gate in the recessed corner ahead. Continue with a curved hedge on your right, step across a stream and climb up the right-hand edge of a narrow field to the A40 road. Turn right along its pavement until the pub is on your left, then cross the road carefully to return to it.

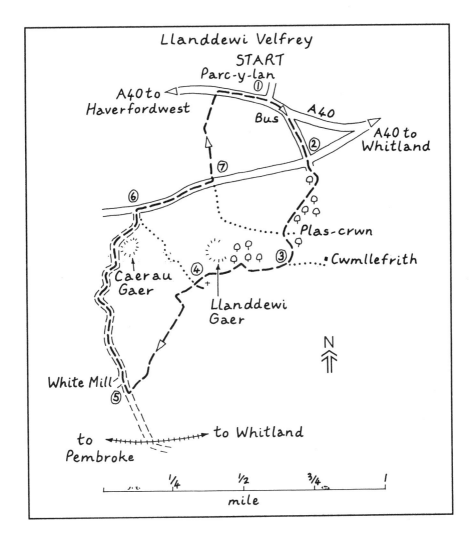

15. Little Haven

Route: Little Haven – Pembrokeshire Coast Path – Musselwick Bay – Woodlands – Little Haven.

Distance: 3 miles. Moderate.

Map: OS Pathfinder 1079 (Haverfordwest.

Start: The Swan Inn, Haverfordwest (SM 856129).

Access: Little Haven is on the coast 1 mile south of Broad Haven, which is at the western end of the B4341 from Haverfordwest. There is an infrequent weekday bus service to Little Haven from Haverfordwest (no. 311). The bus shelter is on the hill to the north of the village.

The Swan Inn, Little Haven (0437 781256)

This is a good socialist pub, previously patronised by Hugh Gaitskill and George Brown, both potential labour Prime Ministers before the premiership of Harold Wilson in the 1960s (when England won the World Cup). Norman Parkinson, the fashion photographer, and Freddie Jones, the actor, have also supped here. Real ale if served while the food is acclaimed (please give advance notice if you require vegetarian dishes). The warm atmosphere is based on a record of hospitality dating back to at least 1785. Opening hours are 11 am to 3 pm and 6.30 pm to 11 pm on weekdays, noon to 3 pm and 7 pm to 10.30 pm on Sundays.

Little Haven

At the time of the Battle of Waterloo this was a coal mining district, with five working collieries. The natural harbour was provided with a local export to supplement fishing. Now it is a favourite beauty spot, with sun-bathers on the former 'loading beach'. The boats were beached as the tide ebbed, loaded with coal at low tide and floated off as the tide rose.

The Swan Inn, Little Haven

The line of the cliffs going west from Musselwick bay betrays a fault
which put ancient volcanic rocks (dating from 1000 million years ago) on
top of more recent coal measures (about 280 million years old). Notice
too how the cliffs have vegetation very low down, reflecting the fact that
this shore is protected from high waves.

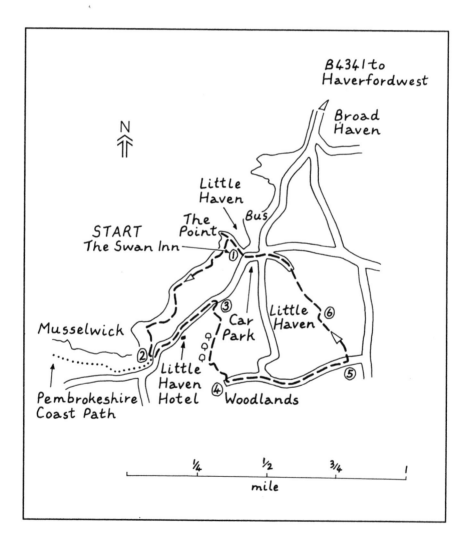

The Walk

1. Go left to follow the Coast Path above the 'haven' on your right. Enjoy the view from the Point before taking the steps up the cliff. Continue along the cliff top Coast Path above the sea on your right.

2. Reach a small car park on your left, with a fine view over Musselwick Bay on your right. Turn left here to join the road and go left along it to pass the Little Haven Hotel on your right.

3. Look out for Glen Court on your left and Rookery Nook on your right. Turn sharply right down a track to pass a private children's playground on your left. Turn left, as signposted, to cross a footbridge and take the waymarked path which soon bears right between trees. Eventually this turns left uphill to reach a lane at Woodvale Bungalow.

4. Go left along the lane to pass Woodlands Cottage on your left. Pass another lane on your left and go ahead until a public footpath signpost beside a kissing gate on your left.

5. Strike out down the field and enter a gully to walk with a stream on your right. Look for a waymarked stile on the other side of the stream and bear right to cross it.

6. Bear left down a long, narrow, field, with the stream away to your left. Leave it by its bottom right-hand corner where a stone stile beside a gate gives access to Wesley Road. Continue along Grove Place to pass the car park and RNLI information centre on your left, Go ahead past the Green and the beach on your right to return to the Swan Inn.

16. Haverfordwest

Route: Haverfordwest – Lower Haroldston – Black Hill -Haverfordwest.

Distance: 5 miles. Easy.

Map: OS Pathfinder 1079 (Haverfordwest).

Start: The Bristol Trader Inn, Haverfordwest (SM 955155).

Access: Haverfordwest is on the A40 between Carmarthen and Fishguard. Trains to its station run from Milford Haven, Carmarthen, Swansea and Cardiff, while there are several local bus services, including numbers 340 from St David's, 358 from Tenby via Pembroke, 381 from Tenby via Narberth and 412 from Cardigan via Fishguard.

The Bristol Trader Inn, Haverfordwest (0437 762122)

Haverfordwest aspired to rival Bristol as a port until the 19th century and the coming of Brunel's railway. This pub has served the needs of Haverfordwest's quay-side for centuries, probably since the French burnt the old port in 1405. The boats that tied up outside the pub door traded much further than Bristol, with Newfoundland, Spain, Portugal and France popular destinations.

The place became notorious for pirates, with the Burgesses taking a percentage from the sale of their ill-gotten gains. Captain Bartholomew Roberts was a successful local pirate who ranked alongside the infamous Morgan. Not surprisingly, this pub has a resident ghost. one of the beds upstairs attracts the ghost of a lady in a crinoline dress and a frilly bonnet. Bed and breakfast accommodation isn't available, so you can't plan to enjoy her company. Real ale and food are available, however, and morning coffee is served. Opening hours are 11 am to 11 pm on weekdays, noon to 3 pm and 7 pm to 10.30 pm on Sundays.

The path through the woodsed slopes above the Western Cleddau

Haverfordwest

The start of this walk highlights the trading tradition of Haverfordwest. Welsh wool was a prime export, as were hides and salted herrings. The resident merchants could afford to import wines and brandy. Visiting boats weren't always so friendly. The Vikings came here in the eighth century and decided to settle. They may have given the place the name of Haver Fjord, meaning 'corn inlet'. The Welsh name is derived from it, being Hwllfford. This may just be a corruption of the Old English HeaferFord (with heafer meaning a buck or he-goat). The addition of 'West' distinguished it from Hertford and Hereford. The Normans made it a key port of their 11th century colony. A fine priory was established by 1200. It was valued at £133 11s 1d when Henry VIII dissolved the monasteries in 1536. The castle was mentioned by Giraldus Cambrensis in 1188 and it wasn't taken by the Welsh when Llywelyn the Great burnt the town in 1200. The French invaders of 1405 left the castle defenders to hide behind their walls as they burnt the town and laid waste the countryside. They were supporting the Welsh Patriot Owain Glyndwr. Henry VII's visit in 1485 on his way to victory at Bosworth was a more agreeable event. The castle finally succumbed to Cromwell, who slighted it before charging the town £25 to cover the cost of doing so.

The Walk

1. From the riverside terrace of the Bristol Trader Inn, go right to walk with the river on your left. Continue along the pavement until the road starts to bend right. Bear left to cross a stone step stile beside a gate and pass the remains of the priory. Continue through a kissing gate and aim for the far corner of the next field, where a stile gives access to the A4076 road on your left. Cross both this road and the subsequent railway with care. Bear right to reach the minor road.

2. Go left along the minor road, cross the bridge over Merlin's Brook and turn left over a stile to follow a signposted public footpath. Soon turn right and walk up the right-hand edge of a second, narrow, field. Enter a third field and turn left to walk with a hedge on your left.

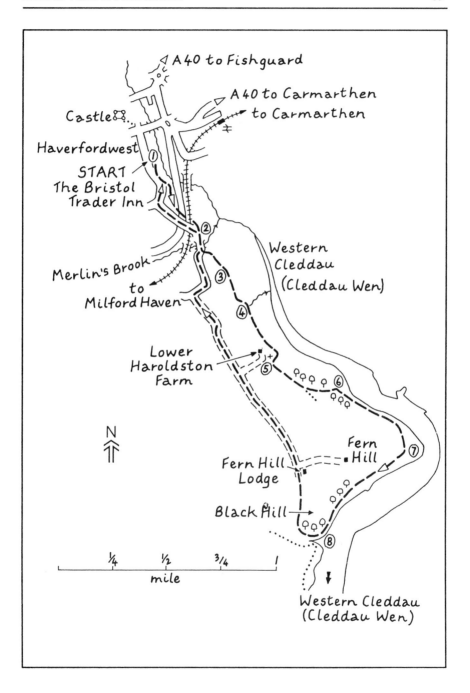

3. Bear left over a stile in the hedge and continue with the hedge on your right. Reach a corner and turn left down the slope beside a hedge on your right.

4. At the foot of the slope turn right over a stile and cross a footbridge over a stream. Bear left, as waymarked by yellow arrows, above the river's flood plain on your left. Go ahead over a stile beside a gate and turn right up the slope, passing the old church dedicated to St Issell on your right.

5. Turn left along a track and continue over a stile beside a gate into woodland. When this track starts to ascend, bear left over a waymarked stile and follow the path through scrub to another stile. Go ahead over this and along a fenced path to a stile which you bear left over to descend through woodland.

6. Walk along the foot of the wooded slope, keeping above the river on your left. The route is waymarked with yellow arrows and new stiles have been erected along it. Eventually descend to the level of the river and follow a hedge on your right. The river makes a sweeping bend away to your left, providing a habit for wildfowl and waders.

7. Bear right through a gap in the hedge to walk with it on your left along the foot of the field. Go ahead over a stile and through woodland. Climb to a field, bear left and reach a derelict building. Bear left down to a stile at the level of the river. Go ahead with the river on your left.

8. Turn away from the river to explore a creek. Ignore a footbridge across the stream on your left. Bear right up an old green lane. This becomes a metalled lane from Fern Hill Lodge. Follow it past the access lane to Lower Haroldston Farm on your right. Turn right at a T-junction with a road. Follow the road across a bridge over the railway and the A4076. Bear right at a fork to descend with the pavement, passing above the old priory ruins. Take the riverside promenade to return to the terrace of the Bristol Trader Inn.

17. Hook

Route: Hook – Western Cleddau Foreshore – Underwood – Hook.

Distance: $3^1/_2$ miles (plus 1 mile each way for optional link with Walk 21). Easy.

Map: OS Pathfinder 1079 (Haverfordwest).

Start: The New Anchor Inn, Hook (SM 969115).

Access: Hook is on a minor road 1 mile east of Freystrop, the crossroads 3 miles south of Haverfordwest. Bus no. 358 runs through Hook on its way between Haverfordwest and Carmarthen, via Pembroke.

The New Anchor Inn, Hook (0437 891343)

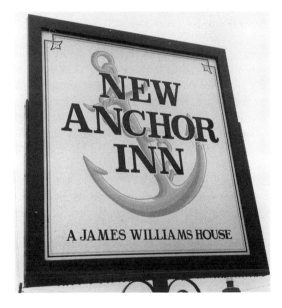

One of the buildings lining the foreshore of the Western Cleddau at the foot of the wooded slope behind this pub used to be the Anchor Inn. The pub migrated to the higher road side in the 1960s, using a converted house. Despite its lack of years, this pub does have a poltergeist. Real ale and food are served. Opening hours are 11 am to 11 pm on weekdays, noon to 3 pm and 7 pm to 10.30 pm on Sundays.

Hook

This wasn't always a haven of rural tranquillity above the wooded slopes of the Western Cleddau. Hook was a busy mining village until surprisingly recently – the last colliery didn't close until 1948. Apart from the riverside quays, there was a rail link with the mainline at Johnston (built as recently as 1929). Production peaked at 42,000 tons in 1934. Closure was hastened by a severe flood. Floods can mean a change of route for this walk (see direction 2). When they recede, the mud-flats and creeks are a naturalist's paradise.

The Walk

1. Go right and pass two bungalows on your right. Immediately after the second of these (no. 86, St Brendon), turn right along a narrow hedged path to the woods. Bear left down a path between conifer trees. Reach another path at a waymark post and turn right to go straight down to a valley track, descending past broad-leaved trees on your left and conifers on your right.

2. Turn right along the valley track. Pass a couple of isolated houses on your right. The broad expanse of water that is the Western Cleddau is on your left. Go ahead along a softer path. *Normally*, it is possible to take the bridleway along the foreshore, between the river on your left and the wooded slope on your right. This passes a *white house* on your right. If there is *exceptionally* high flooding, do not try to walk along the foreshore this side of the *white house*. Bear right instead up a woodland path to the road. Bear left until the start of Greenway Close, Hook, but turn left down a rough track. This zig-zags to the *white house*. Continue along the foreshore, passing the white house on your right, with the Western Cleddau on your left. Eventually the wooded slope on your right comes to an end.

3. When you reach Underwood Cottage, turn sharply right along its access lane. Reach a junction with a minor road.

4. *If you are Linking this route with Walk 21 (Llangwm),* turn left along the road, which bends to the right before a final bend on your left into

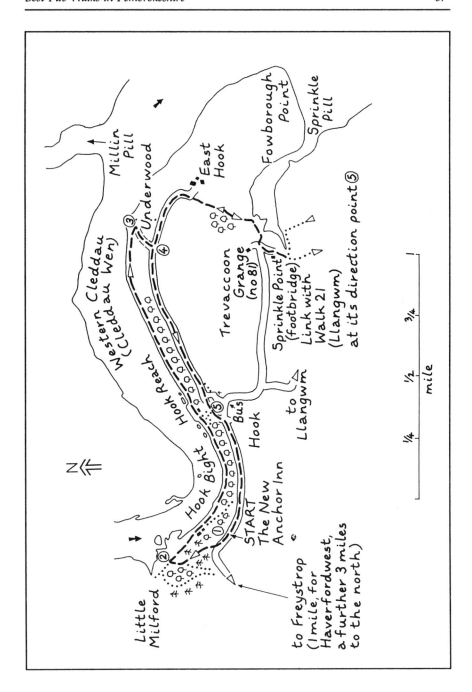

East Hook. Do not take this final bend on your left. Go straight ahead over a stile beside a gate to follow the signposted bridleway, which is an old green lane. Emerge through a gate at its end. Bear right, keeping Sprinkle Pill on your left. Bear right up a creek to step across the streams feeding the creek and reach a roadside signpost. Turn left along a road giving access to a house named Sprinkle Point. Go ahead along a path which passes this house on your right. This leads to the footbridge which is direction point 5 of Walk 21 (Llangwm).

If you are continuing this route (Walk 17, Hook), turn right along the road. This passes above the wooded slope and the Western Cleddau on your right. When, after one mile, this road eventually turns left into Hook (it passes a United Reformed Church on your left and joins the main road through the village opposite the bus shelter), maintain your direction by taking the track ahead. Continue along a hedged path to join a track ascending through the woodland (from the white house).

5. Go left to reach the main road and turn right along it, keeping above the trees and the river on your right, to return to the New Anchor Inn, on your right.

18. Marloes

Route: Marloes – Marloes Sands – Pembrokeshire Coast Path -Deer Park – Pembrokeshire Coast Path – Musselwick Sands – Marloes.

Distance: 7 miles. Moderate.

Map: OS Pathfinder 1102 (Skomer Island).

Start: The Lobster Pot Inn, Marloes (SM 792085).

Access: Marloes is just over 1 mile to the west of the B4327 road as it approaches Dale, about 12 miles west-south-west of Haverfordwest. Bus no. 315 runs to Marloes from Haverfordwest on Tuesdays, with bus no. 316 connecting the two places on Fridays.

The Lobster Pot Inn, Marloes (0646 636233)

Lord Kensington closed all the pubs in this village in the 19th century. The place remained dry until 1963, when this pub was built (the restaurant next door occupies a former cottage). The restaurant is famous for its local seafood and is open from 7 pm each evening. Vegetarian and vegan dishes are available, while special diets can be catered for on an individual basis. The pub serves food between 11 am and 3 pm and 7 pm to 10.30 pm on Sundays. Breakfasts and packed luncheons for walkers are served from 8 am to 10 am. Despite being new, the pub has acquired an atmosphere, helped by a welcoming open fire. Perhaps you'll be as lucky as the regulars who shared a pools win of £32,000 in the early 1970s. If you're taking a trip to Ireland from Fishguard, this pub is 'twinned' with another Lobster Pot at Carne, near Rosslare.

Marloes Peninsula

Peninsulas seem to be special places. The ancients may have recognised some property to do with the spirit, as if the life-force converges on the point. The souls of the dead were associated with off-shore islands and it is interesting to note that cairn circles were erected for some reason on

Skomer Island. The Deer Park (which never contained deer) was marked off in prehistory by a mighty earthwork. This is counted as a defensive structure but such ramparts may have been started for religious reasons. A link with religion was provided by the discovery of a stone cross (marking a prayer station?) when the public toilets were built in the 1980s. It has been dated to the period between AD 600 and 900. Even the 'side peninsula' of Gateholm (an island at high tide) bears the remains of an early Celtic Christian religious settlement (the terms 'monastery' might only serve to confuse with much later, different, establishments). Albion Sands, to the west of Gateholm, are named after the *Albion*, an early paddle-steamer which was wrecked here in 1837.

Come here in the autumn and you may see grey seals and their pups. This peninsula and, particularly, Skomer Island, are important seal-breeding sites.

The Lobster Pot

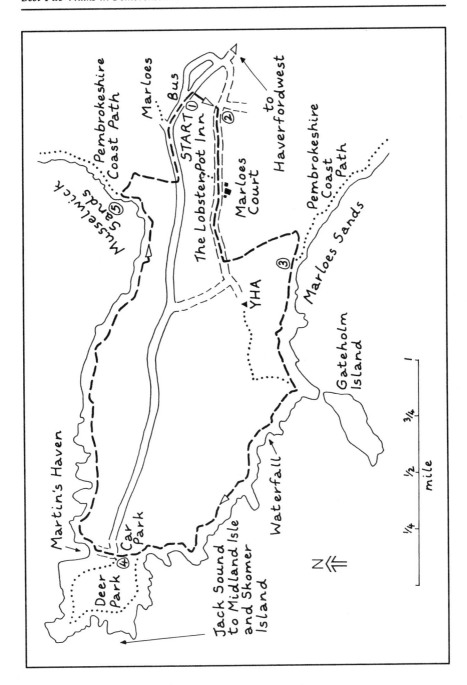

The Walk

1. Go right and approach the Clock Tower on your left. Turn right to take the signposted public footpath which passes behind the Foxes Inn and continues as a hedged path.

2. Turn right along a metalled lane. Ignore a waymarked stile on your right just before you pass Marloes Court on your left. Turn left when you come to a path signposted for 'The Beach 700m'.

3. Turn right along the Coast Path to walk above the sea on your left. Eventually cross a stile to enter the Deer park at the tip of the peninsula, with Midland Isle and Skomer Island ahead, across Jack Sound. The Coast Path signpost directs you inland to walk with the Deer Park's wall on your right. It is possible to continue around the headland, following well-trodden paths and bearing right as you descend from the Coast Guard look-out to reach the stile beside a gate in the Deer Park's wall.

4. Cross the stile beside the gate in the Deer Park's wall and turn left, as signposted, to pass the Skomer Marine Nature Reserve Office and public toilets on your left. Immediately after these buildings, notice an old cross set in the wall on your left. Go ahead towards where the seasonal ferry to Skomer goes from and turn right to follow the signposted Coast Path. Keep above the sea on your left for $2^1/2$ miles, until you are above Musselwick Sands.

5. Approach the aptly-names Black Cliff and turn right along the signposted public footpath going inland. Join a farm track which comes through a gate on your left and bear right along the left-hand edge of a field. Go ahead over a stile to reach a road and turn left along it back into Marloes and the Lobster Pot Inn.

19. Robeston Wathen

Route: The Bridge Inn — Robeston Wathen — Canaston Wood — The Knights' Way — Canaston Bridge — The Landsker Borderlands Trail — Llawhaden — Robeston Wathen — The Bridge Inn.

Distance: 7^1/$_2$ miles. Easy.

Map: OS Pathfinder 1080 (Narberth).

Start: The Bridge Inn, Robeston Wathen (SN 094155).

Access: The Bridge Inn is on the B4314 road ^{1}/$_2$ a mile east of the A40 at Robeston Wathen, where there is a bus stop for numbers 322 (Haverfordwest-Narberth-Carmarthen) and 381 (Haverfordwest-Narberth-Tenby). The Bridge Inn is 1^1/$_2$ miles west of Narberth, which has a railway station as well as bus services.

The Bridge Inn, Robeston Wathen (0834 860541)

This was called the Dick Turpin Inn until 1991. Tastefully decorated and adorned with rugby memorabilia, the pub boasts a resident ghost. Real ale, food and morning coffee are served. Opening hours are 11 am to 11 pm on weekdays, noon to 3 pm and 7 pm to 10.30 pm on Sundays.

Robeston Wathen

The place name refers to Robert, a sub-tenant of the Norman Lord of Narberth, and to the Wadyn family. Turnpike roads with toll-gates ran through here and a toll-gate at the east end of the village was attacked by the Rebecca Rioters in 1843. The hill top church at the centre of so many tracks, lanes and roads is, appropriately known as the church of the Holy Cross. Its 13th century tower can be seen for miles around. The rest of the church was rebuilt in the late 19th century by Sir Thomas Jackson, who built the Examination Schools at Oxford University.

Canaston Wood and the Knights' Way

The ancient forest was comprised of oak and hazel but exotic larch and spruce trees were planted in the 1950s by the Forestry Commission. There is evidence of coppicing, while beech trees have been planted alongside the old unclassified county road which forms part of the Knights' Way. This 9 mile route connects the Pembrokeshire Coast Path at Amroth with the Landsker Borderlands Trail near Canaston Bridge. Waymarked in black and white with a Maltese cross (as worn by the medieval Knights Hospitallers of St John) this route leads towards the Hospitallers' base at Slebech, across the Eastern Cleddau. Pilgrims on their way to St David's came here, while Slebech also served as a hospital for the infirm and as a recruitment centre for the Crusades.

The Landsker Borderlands Trail and Llawhaden

The Landsker was the imaginary frontier between English and Welsh speakers in Pembrokeshire/Preseli (although the word is of Norse origin). This trail provides a 60 mile walking route around the area, with a distinctive purple waymark. It goes through the village of Llawhaden, where there is a ruined castle, the remains of a medieval hospice chapel and a Norman church.

The Walk

1. Go left up the road to Robeston Wathen, bearing left along the pavement when you reach the A40. Pass a garage on your left, then Church Lane on your right. Turn left down the lane opposite the bus shelter. This is soon signed as 'Unsuitable for Motors'. When this lane approaches a ford, at the bottom of the valley, take a stile in the hedge on your right to cut across a field to a footbridge which crosses the stream to the right of the ford. Continue along the lane.

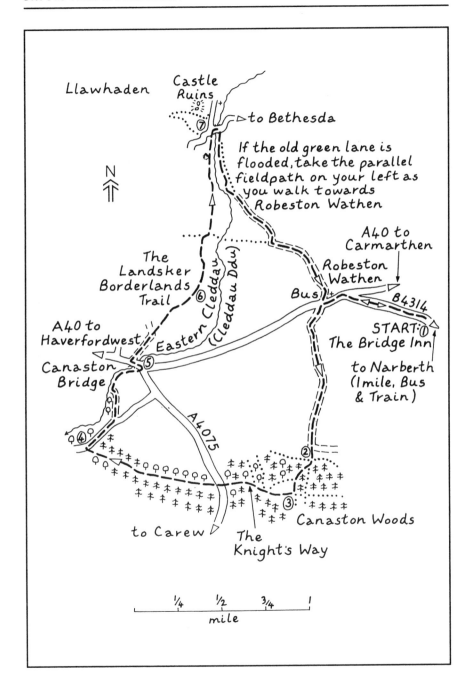

2. When the lane bends left, go straight ahead along a signposted bridleway. Enter Canaston Wood through a small gate and take the signposted bridleway which bears slightly to the right as it climbs through the wood, passing conifer trees on your left and deciduous on your right.

3. Turn right along the firm track which is waymarked as the Knight's Way. Continue with it across the A4075.

4. Turn right along a minor road. Fork left as waymarked for the Landsker Borderlands Trail, crossing a cattle grid and following a lane. Bear left near its end through a gate into woodland and go ahead to the river (the Eastern Cleddau). Turn right to walk with the river on your left. Go ahead over a stile, along the left-hand edge of a field and through a small gate ahead. Cross the subsequent footbridge and bear right through a car park to reach the A40 at its junction with the A4075.

5. Turn left with the pavement across Canaston Bridge, then turn right to cross the A40 with care and go ahead along the signposted Landsker Borderlands Trail. This begins as a metalled lane but when it bends left through a gate, bear right through a field-gate and walk, as signposted, beside a hedge on your right. Keep it there as you go ahead through a gate into the next field, then again into a third field.

6. Bear right through a gate in the hedge on your right in this third field. Contour around the field to eventually join a track running beside a hedge on your right. Take a gate in the corner and follow the waymarked route through a farmyard. Continue along the foot of a wooded slope. Pass below Pen-yr-allt and above the river. Reach a road at the edge of Llawhaden and go right along it.

7. Turn right across Llawhaden Bridge (a substantial stone structure). Turn right immediately after it to follow the signposted bridleway, with the river now on your right. If this old green lane is flooded, take the waymarked public footpath which runs parallel to it through fields on your left. This eventually crosses a footbridge to rejoin the old green lane. Go left up a drier track which becomes a metalled lane and leads back into Robeston Wathen as Church Lane. Go left along the pavement of the A40 and soon fork right down the B4314 to return to the Bridge Inn.

20. Narberth

Route: Narberth – Pitch Cross – The Knights' Way – Narberth.

Distance: 6 miles. Moderate.

Map: OS Pathfinder 1080 (Narberth).

Start: The Angel, Narberth (SN 109147).

Access: Narberth is near the junction of the A40 with the A478. Trains run to its railway station from Cardiff, Swansea, Carmarthen, Tenby and Pembroke. Bus services to Narberth include the no. 322 (Haverfordwest-Carmarthen) and no. 381 (Tenby-Haverfordwest).

The Angel, Narberth (0834 860574)

French prisoners from the farcical invasion at Carregwastad Point in 1797 (see Walk No. 3 Fishguard) were kept upstairs here for while, while the resident ghost is of a woman in the dress of that period. No strong drink would have been served to them as this place was founded as a Temperance Hotel in the 18th century (hence the name). Real ale and food are served today, while there is a beer garden. Opening hours are 11 am to 3 pm and 5.30 pm to 11 pm on weekdays, noon to 3 pm and 7 pm to 10.30 pm on Sundays.

Narberth

This is a magical little town whose past is well-recorded in the Landsker Visitor Centre. The ancient Celtic Kingdom of Dyfed was ruled from here and its castle (the ruins are Norman) most probably marks the site of the Court of Pwyll outside which Rhiannon had to do penance (unfairly), as recounted in *The Mabinogion*. Learn too about the Rebecca Riots in the Visitor Centre. Narberth's history makes it a focal point for old tracks, including the delightful Carding Mill Lane which forms the final leg of this route. The Templars and the Knights' Hospitallers of St John rode this way in the Middle Ages, when this was border country (the Norse word 'Landsker' means frontier) between Welsh and English. The Knights' Way is now a walking route linking the south-eastern end of the Pembrokeshire Coast Path at Amroth with the upper tidal reaches of the Eastern Cleddau at Blackpool Mill, where it meets the Daugleddau Trail. The Knights Templar wore a white mantle over their armour marked with a red cross, while the Hospitallers were distinguished by a white eight-pointed cross on a black mantle, as is used to waymark the modern walking route.

Narberth was a centre for cattle drovers and even after the advent of the railway some markets would see 1000 cattle for sale and being driven through the town to the railway station after being sold. Near the market square is The Wilson Museum of Narberth, with is also well worth a visit, if only to see how the local beer used to be brewed and bottled.

Narberth is now home to the South Pembrokeshire Partnership for Action with Rural Communities (SPARC), housed in the Old School, Station Road (tel. 0834 860965). Ask for details of its walking programmes and leaflets.

The Walk

1. Go right, down the High Street and pass the Landsker Visitor Centre on your right. Continue past the market cross on your left to reach the castle ruins.

2. Facing the signposted path up to the castle ruins, go left and soon turn right with a signposted public footpath which passes below the castle ruins, on your right. Turn left to cross a footbridge and reach a stone step stile in the top corner. Turn right to cross it and turn left to continue over a wooden step stile shortly after it. Cross a field to a waymarked stile which is in the hedge on your right about 50 yards short of the corner ahead. Maintain this direction to take a stile beside a gate and follow an enclosed path to a farmhouse.

3. Go left along a firm track. Turn right at a cross-tracks, cross a stream and go left along a valley lane. Fork left with a muddy track before the lane climbs to bear right for Forest Farm.

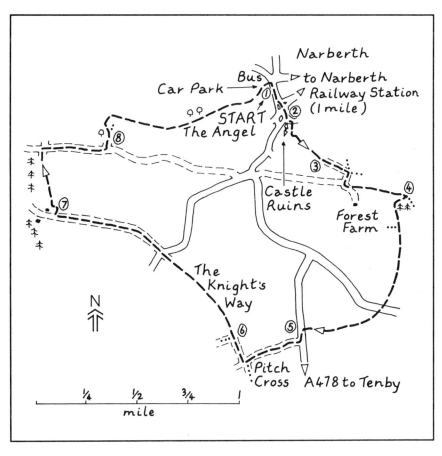

4. Turn sharply right up a track which soon bears left out of a patch of woodland as an old green lane. Follow it to a road, which you cross to continue along the track ahead (signposted as a public footpath). This bears right to reach the A478.

5. Go left along the verge of the A478 for 50 yards, then turn right along a rough lane. Turn right at a cross-tracks (Pitch Cross).

6. When the main track turns left at another junction, go straight ahead. This is the waymarked Knights' Way. Follow this route across a road and along a lane for half a mile.

7. Just before the lane descends to a farm, turn right through a hunting gate and join a broad, hedged, track which descends past woodland on your left to a valley road. Turn right along this road, ignoring the track ahead signposted to Returno.

8. At a signposted junction named 'Shipping Factory', turn left along a rough lane. Bear left, as waymarked at a fork. Cross a stream by a concrete bridge and follow a delightful hedged track (Carding Mill Lane) as it bears right back to Narberth. Pass the car park, a school and a bus shelter, then turn right down the High Street to find The Angel on your right.

The Angel

21. Llangwm

Route: Llangwm – Sprinkle Farm – Sprinkle Point – Llangwm.

Distance: $3^1/_2$ miles (plus 1 mile each way for optional link with Walk 17). Moderate.

Map: OS Pathfinder 1079 (Haverfordwest) and 1103 (Milford Haven).

Start: The Cottage Inn, Llangwm (SM 989096).

Access: Llangwm is on a minor road 3 miles east of Freystrop, the crossroads 3 miles south of Haverfordwest. Bus no. 358 runs through Llangwm on its way between Haverfordwest and Carmarthen via Pembroke.

The Cottage Inn, Llangwm (0437 891494)

This was a 'dry' village from the 19th century until the coronation of Queen Elizabeth II. A stabbing after the haymakers celebrated the end of their work with a drink or two gave the local land owner, who was a total abstainer, reason to close the old village pub. Eventually, in 1953, a bakehouse became the Cottage Club, serving members with alcoholic drinks. This swiftly graduated to becoming a pub. It now serves real ale and bar snacks and has a restaurant. Opening hours are 11 am to 3 pm

and 5 pm to 11 pm from Monday to Wednesday during the Summer (noon to 3 pm and 5.30 pm to 11 pm during the winter), 11 am to 11 pm from Thursday to Saturday (noon to 11 pm during the Winter) and noon to 3 pm, then 7 pm to 10.30 pm on Sundays.

Llangwm

The road network still hardly recognises Llangwm. In the past it isolated the place, turning it towards the river estuary and the sea for communications. Coal used to be exported from Llangwm Pill and Sprinkle Pill, while fishing was a major concern.

Salmon were – still are – caught by compass netting, where a net is fixed between two poles. It was said that the maritime connections and the insularity encouraged aggressive attitudes in the locals, with the women being notorious for their violence. Perhaps this traditional view deserves to be discussed over a pint with the locals.

The Walk

1. Bear left through the village. Pass the bus shelter on your right. Turn left just before the road descends to a bridge. Follow Rectory Road above Llangwm Pill on your right.

2. Ignore Glan Hafan on your left. Continue along the lane above Llangwm Pill, then Edward's Pill, on your right. Turn right over a bridge at the head of Edward's Pill and climb with a signposted public footpath which begins as a metalled lane.

3. Bear left through a metal kissing-gate to take the signposted public footpath across a field. Continue over a stile in the hedge opposite to gain access to a lane. Turn left up this, passing Knapp Farm on your right.

4. Turn right along the signposted bridleway at Sprinkle Farm. This passes farm buildings on your right and follows a hedge on your left. Continue along a wide, hedged, track. Descend with this to two field gates. Go ahead through the left-hand gate and descend to the foot of this field. Turn left to walk with the bottom fence on your right. Step across a steam and a low (non-barbed) wire fence in the corner. Go ahead 10 yards in the next field to reach a stile giving access to a footbridge on your right.

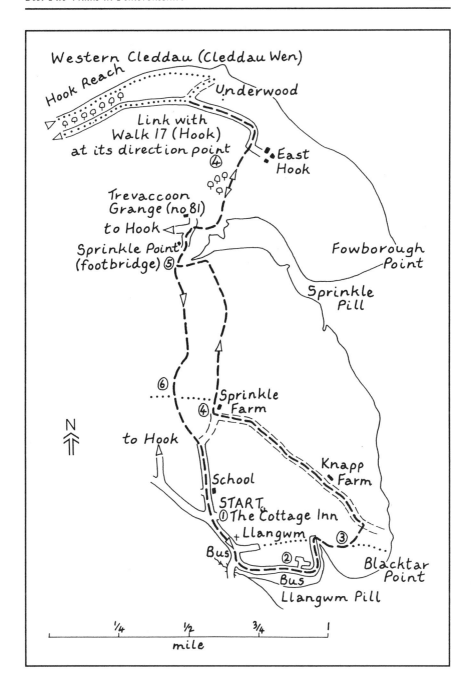

5. *If you are linking this route with Walk 17 (Hook)*, turn right over the stile and footbridge. Follow a path ahead to join the access drive from a house called Sprinkle Point. Continue to a road junction and bear right along a signposted public footpath. Take a gate on your left to go up an old green lane which leads to a road. Go straight ahead along this road (not right, for East Hook) and turn left with it to reach direction point 4 of Walk 17 (Hook).

If you are continuing this route, do NOT turn right over the stile and footbridge. Instead, place your back towards them and go ahead up the pasture with a hedge on your left. Go ahead over a waymarked stile in the top left corner and continue beside a hedge on your left. Continue across a stile in the next corner and along an old green lane.

6. Another hedged path converges with yours from the right. Bear slightly left as you continue to the lane. Turn right along the lane to enter Llangwm. Pass the school on your left. Approach a road junction and bear left back to the Cottage Inn.

22. Dale

Route: Dale – Dale Fort – Pembrokeshire Coast Path – St Ann's Head – Pembrokeshire Coast Path – Westdale Bay – Dale.

Distance: 7 miles. Moderate.

Map: OS Pathfinder 1102 (Skomer Island) and 1103 (Milford Haven).

Start: The Griffin Inn, Dale (SM 812057).

Access: Dale is at the end of the B4327 about 123 miles south-west of Haverfordwest, from where the numbers 315 and 316 buses run on Tuesdays and Fridays.

The Griffin Inn, Dale (0646 636227)

This old sailors' haunt was once the village brewery. Sup here of an evening and you may enjoy the company of a real lighthouse keeper. The griffin on the counter was carved from driftwood by a local man. There is a cosy fire downstairs but a ghost of a dog can be heard padding about upstairs. Some people also report seeing the ghost of a woman at an upstairs window. As bed and breakfast isn't available here (but plentiful elsewhere in the village), you'll have to stand outside gazing at the windows for a glimpse of her. Over 30 malt whiskies are available, as are real ales and food, including vegetarian dishes. Opening hours are 11 am to 11 pm on weekdays, noon to 3 pm and 7 pm to 10.30 pm on Sundays.

Dale

The place name shows that we're south of the Landsker – Dale is derived from the Norse word for a valley. The sunniest place in Wales, it has long been known as a good area for growing crops. Such a valuable spot had to be well defended, with the old castle (really a fortified manor house) built originally by Robert de Vale. Dale became a busy little fishing port, trading centre and place where ships were built. Now it is thronged in the summer by sailing and surfing enthusiasts. It has long held a strategic post on the coastline. The tip of its peninsula is now dedicated to St Ann but the name may reflect an earlier devotion to 'tan' (Welsh for fire). Perhaps beacons were lit here in ancient times, if only at Beltane (May 1st).

Since 1800 there has been a lighthouse on this site, with the current model erected in 1841. Coastal and maritime rescues are also co-ordinated from here. Fear of French invasion caused the Victorians to build the West Blockhouse. Dale Fort was built in 1856 and is now a field centre for marine biologists.

August 7th, 1485, gave the Dale Peninsula the right to claim its place in British history alongside such places as Pevensey, near Hastings (where William the Conqueror landed in 1066). The greatest British dynasty launched its claim to the throne here. Henry Tudor, the future King Henry VII, landed with 2000 followers from Brittany, on his way to earn the crown by defeating King Richard III at the Battle of Bosworth. Henry came with a sense of destiny, believing he was about to restore the golden age of King Arthur, who is now known to have finished his days and have been buried as St Arthmael in Brittany, where Henry Tudor lived in exile and set out for Dale from. Read *Journey to Avalon* by Chris Barber and David Pykitt (Blorenge Books, 1993) for more on the link between Henry Tudor and King Arthur. First, however, Henry had to convince Sir Rhys ap Thomas, the ruler of Dyfed, to go against the king he had sworn allegiance to. A Wise Man of Dale advised Sir Rhys that Henry would enjoy success. His rhyming words were:

'Ful well I wend, that in the end
Richmond, sprung from British race,
From out this land, the boare shall chase.'

Henry Tudor was the Earl of Richmond and of ancient British descent (even related to King Arthur), while Richard III's symbol was a boar. Sir Rhys satisfied his conscience by lying beneath Mullock Bridge while Henry Tudor, his men plus 8000 of Rhys' men crossed it. Sir Rhys had sworn to permit no landing 'except over his body'.

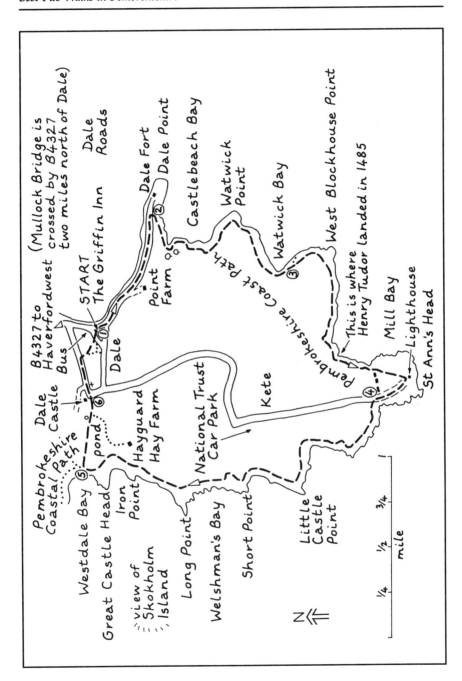

The Walk

1. Go right along the road to Dale Fort and Point. Pass Dale Yacht Club on your right and climb above the sea on your left. Pass the access lane to Point Farm on your right. Approach Dale Fort Field Centre but turn right 200 yards before it, crossing a stile waymarked with an acorn symbol. Go ahead towards Castlebeach Bay.

2. Bear right over a stile to follow the Coast Path, keeping the sea on your left. The Coast Path is well-waymarked and signposted, with stiles where necessary. Pass Watwick Beacon on your left.

3. Ignore a path going down to the sea on your left. Keep to the cliff top path to West Blockhouse Point. Continue along the Coast Path to pass the lighthouse on St Ann's Head on your left. Follow its access road past a radio mast on your left.

On the coast path above Westdale Bay

4. Leave the road (which continues to Dale), by turning left over a stile and along the signposted Coast Path. Keep the sea on your left and ignore waymarked stiles on your right which serve the National Trust's car park at Kete. You will be alerted to your exit from the Coast Path by passing Hayguard Hay Farm on your right and gaining a view over to Dale. The Coast Path then cuts across the neck of Great Castle Head on your left to overlook Westdale Bay. Go down steps.

5. Turn right over a stone step stile to take the signposted valley path back to Dale. Go ahead over a stile to the right of a gate and a pond to walk below Dale Castle on your left. Follow a farm track to a road.

6. Take the road ahead to pass the Church of St James the Great on your right. Ignore a No Through Road on your left. Turn right over a stone step stile to take a signposted public footpath across a meadow. Bear left over a stile beside a gate in the middle of the meadow and reach a road. Cross it to follow a metalled footpath past public toilets on your left. Emerge facing the sea and with the Coronation Hall on your right. Bear right past this to return to the Griffin Inn.

23. Saundersfoot

Route: Saundersfoot – Wiseman's Bridge – Pleasant Valley -Stepaside Bird and Animal Park – Grove Colliery – Saundersfoot.

Distance: 5 miles. Moderate.

Map: OS Pathfinder 1104 (Tenby).

Start: Royal Oak Inn, Saundersfoot (SN 136049).

Access: Saundersfoot has a railway station on the line between Carmarthen and Pembroke over a mile inland of the resort. The centre of Saundersfoot is served by buses numbers 351 (Tenby-Amroth), 358 and 359 (Haverfordwest-Tenby-Carmarthen), 361 (Pembroke-Tenby) and 381 (Haverfordwest-Narberth-Tenby).

Royal Oak Inn (0834 813675)

Nick Owen of Breakfast TV and other media personalities sup here, so the food and real ale must be up to standard. Opening hours of this old pub are 11 am to 11 pm on weekdays, noon to 3 pm and 7 pm to 10.30 pm on Sundays.

Saundersfoot

Tourism is the mainstay of the local economy today, but this used to be a heavy industrial area. The revolution came in the early 19th century with Saundersfoot rapidly expanding from the eight houses that comprised it in 1810 (only two houses in 1764). The local anthracite coal, which had previously been exported from the beach at Wiseman's Bridge, was shipped from Saundersfoot's new harbour after its construction in 1829. The total exported grew from 11,500 tons in 1833 to 38,600 tons in 1864. Much of this walk's route is along the course of the dismantled colliery tramway between Saundersfoot and Stepaside. Stepaside Ironworks were opened in 1849, using coal from the nearby

Grove Colliery. Production ceased in 1877. Wiseman's Bridge was famous for its production of excellent fire bricks in 1850.

The beach at Saundersfoot

Shipwreck!

A strong south-westerly gale on Sunday night, 7th December 1856 caused the Tenby Lifeboat with its crew of 12 to stand ready for the call that duly came. The square rigged Spanish barque called *Nuevo Torcuvate* had run aground on a submerged sandbank off-shore from Saundersfoot. it was a difficult rescue, with the seas washing clean over the Spanish vessel's stern, but all 9 crew were successfully taken off. The wrecked ship broke up within two hours of the rescue, for which the gallant crew each received £1 from the National Lifeboat Institution.

The Walk

1. Cross the road and go right to the crossroads, where you turn left to pass the Hean Castle Hotel on your left. Head for the beach and turn left to walk with the sea on your right, or in the event of rough weather and very high tides go left along The Strand. Leave the beach through a gateway near the end of the buildings on your left and turn right to the end of The Strand.

2. Go ahead, as signposted for the toilets, through an old railway tunnel. Emerge at a car park. Cross this, passing its entrance on your left, and follow the signposted Coast Path past Coppet Hall Beach Cafe on your left.

3. Pass the safer alternative Coast Path route which is signposted on your left (or take it in the event of bad weather and high tides). Bear right with a track to follow the Coast Path through a second tunnel and along an old railway above the sea on your right. Go ahead through a third tunnel. Pass the safer alternative Coast Path coming down steps on your left. Continue to the road at Wiseman's Bridge.

4. Cross the road to pass a telephone box on your left and take the elevated metalled lane past Step Cottage on your left, above Wiseman's Bridge on your right. When this lane bears left, go ahead along a track at the foot of the wooded slope of Pleasant Valley. Ignore a stile below on your right, just before the stream returns to accompany you.

5. Go left along a road for half a mile to a junction. Turn sharply left at the Stepaside Craft Village. Follow the signposted public footpath (a track) past the bird and animal park on your right and a railway on your left. Continue above a caravan park on your left and pass the surface remains of Grove Colliery (depth 640ft) on your right. Go ahead over a stile and fork right to climb through the forest to a stile. Cross it and turn right through a paddock to reach a lane.

6. Turn right to a crossroads, where you turn left. Go right when you eventually come to a T-junction and soon fork left. Reach the car park traversed on the outward journey and turn left into it to immediately bear right and retrace your steps through the initial railway tunnel to Saundersfoot and the Royal Oak Inn.

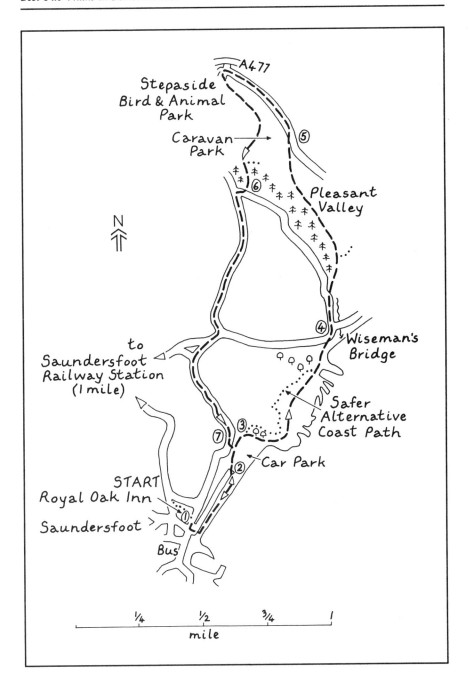

24. Angle

Route: Angle — West Angle Bay — Pembrokeshire Coast Path -Castle Farm — Angle.

Distance: 4 miles. Easy.

Map: OS Pathfinder 1103 (Milford Haven).

Start: Hibernia Inn, Angle (SM 863030).

Access: Angle is at the end of the B4320 road 12 miles west of Pembroke. There is an infrequent bus service (no. 366) to Angle from Pembroke, with nearly all the buses running on Fridays.

Hibernia Inn, Angle (0646 641517)

This pub is closer to Ireland than to England (despite the name of the village). Irish sailors often called here and the pub is named after the Latin name for Ireland. Perhaps some of the regulars were Hibernians (the Nationalist Roman Catholic opposite of the Orange Order, which may have existed at Pembroke – see Walk 25).

The date given inside the pub for its foundation is 1865, although 1866 is on the pub sign. It is anything but Hibernian in character today, with the Battle Ensign of H.M.S. *Conqueror* on display (from the Falklands War, 1982). One room is full of lifeboat memorabilia and the father of the former coxswain of Angle lifeboat has been seen as a ghost, sitting in his old place now partly occupied by a fruit machine. The log fire adds to the atmosphere, while there is a beer garden. Real ale and food are served. Opening hours are 11.30 am to 3 pm and 6.30 pm to 11 pm on weekdays, noon to 3 pm and 7 pm to 10.30 pm on Sundays.

Angle

The Anglo-Norman invaders couldn't feel secure here for centuries – hence the castle (which was more of a fortified manor house). The tower behind the parish church dates from the 14th century and is known as the Old Rectory. It attains a height of 30ft, is well preserved and has three small rooms above a vaulted cellar. A dovecote stands on private land nearby (ask at Castle Farm). The fishermen's chapel at the back of the church dates from 1447. The most surprising building is the isolated hotel on Thorn Island. Perhaps an ideal honeymoon location, this is set in an old Palmerston fort, built to protect the naval dockyard from the threat of French invaders in the mid-19th century. There is now an air of peace here, which makes the sight of the oil refineries across the water even more incongruous. With water on three sides, there is the feel of an island to this route.

The entrance into Angle is past an old world inlet with boats and tidal mudflats for wading birds. This tranquil scene must have been shattered on 30th January, 1894, when the sailing ship *Loch Shiel*, bound from Glasgow to Adelaide, Australia, with over 7000 cases of the finest Scottish Whisky plus bottled beer and all sorts of spirits, was wrecked on Thorn Island. The locals had a true 'Whisky Galore' bonanza and one man died from 'excessive whisky drinking', while two others were drowned as they tried to tow a keg ashore. Customs men discovered over 2000 bottles, but most were concealed and consumed. All 27 people on board of the *Loch Shiel* were successfully rescued by the twelve-oared Angle lifeboat.

The Walk

1. Cross the road to the pavement and turn right. Go ahead all the way to the beach at West Angle, ignoring a road which goes left and Mirehouse Place on your right.

2. Turn right over a stile to follow the signposted Coast Path, keeping the sea on your left. Ignore a fork bearing left, then another on your right. Go ahead as signposted. Climb to a stile beside another signpost and cross it to walk with a fence on your right past Thorn Island' on your left. Continue over two more stiles and past a TV mast.

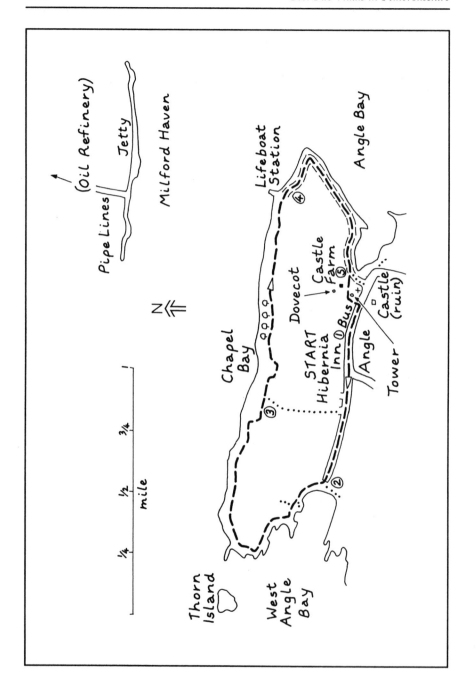

3. Ignore the track going right. Take the track ahead, towards Chapel Bay. When this terminates at a field gate, fork left, as signposted, over a stile. Walk with a hedge on your right and a wooded slope down to the sea on your left. Emerge in the corner of a field with a view of Milford Haven's oil terminals on your left. Go ahead along the left-hand edges of five fields and pass above the lifeboat station before bearing down to its access lane.

4. Go right along the lifeboat station's access lane. Pass the tidal inlet which serves Angle as a harbour for yachts, on your left.

5. Do not bear left towards St Mary's Church, across a stone bridge. Fork right instead to pass a Norman tower on your left. Ask at Castle Farm to divert right and see a Dovecote (on private land). Turn left off the track to take a kissing-gate into the playground beside the school and go ahead to the road.

6. If you wish to visit St Mary's Church (with the fishermen's chapel at its rear) divert left. The castle ruins are ahead, behind the Post Office. Turn right along the road to reach the Hibernia Inn on your right.

Returning to Angle

25. Pembroke

Route: Pembroke – Maiden Wells – Hundleton – Pembrokeshire Coast Path – Pembroke.

Distance: 6 miles. Moderate.

Map: OS Pathfinder 1103 (Milford Haven) and 1124 (Castlemartin & St Govan's Head).

Start: Cromwell's Tavern, Pembroke (SM 988015).

Access: Pembroke is at the western end of the A477 and can be reached by train from Carmarthen. Local buses radiate from the town.

Cromwell's Tavern (0646 682223)

No, this wasn't a pub in Cromwell's day, but the building survived as a private dwelling from the Middle ages until the 20th century, when a cafe known as Cromwell's Kitchen opened in it. It became a pub in the 1970s.

Cromwell's association with Pembroke came in 1648, when he besieged the castle. Civil War memorabilia decorates the travern's walls, while the log fire adds an authentic touch. Steve Fenwick, the Welsh rugby star, has supped here, as did the cast of the film *Jabberwocky* (including Michael Palin) when it was being filmed in the castle. Real ale and food are available. Opening hours are 11 am to 11 pm on weekdays, noon to 3 pm and 7 pm to 10.30 pm on Sundays.

The Priory Inn (0646 684422)

The Salutation Inn used to stand here, before being knocked down and replaced by this pub, which serves bar snacks, in the 1960s. Opening hours are 11 am to 11 pm on weekdays, noon to 3 pm and 7 pm to 10.30 pm on Sundays.

Pembroke

Pembroke Castle is the greatest fortress in Dyfed, at the heart of the Anglo-Norman colony and with access from the sea. Its round keep, inner and outer wards, curtain wall with defensive towers, halls, gatehouse, chancery and chapel make it a classic example of a medieval castle. It is in private hands, so even CADW (Heritage in Wales) members must pay admission. Opening hours are 9.30 am to 5 pm from April to September, 10 am to 5 pm in March and October, then 10 am to 4 pm from November to February. Henry VII, the first Tudor King, was born here, in 1457. West of the castle, and passed by this route, is Monkton Priory Church. Henry VII was educated here by the Benedictine Monks. When Cromwell besieged the castle, he placed his cannon beside the present vicarage. The curate-in-charge remained at his post, despite the noise and danger, and preached to Cromwell's officers.

Pembroke Castle

As you make your way towards Pembroke, notice the sign for the Orange Hall. This may be where Orangemen met in Wales, as they still do today in Northern Ireland, Scotland and Liverpool. Pembroke grew tremendously in importance with the Royal Naval Dockyard being constructed in the early 19th century. The town hasn't really recovered from the dockyard's closure in 1926. In 1875 the Chief Constructor of the American Navy had reported that Pembroke Dockyard was 'the finest ship-building yard in the world'.

The Walk

1. Go left to pass the castle on your right. Take the pavement of the B4320 out of Pembroke, ignoring the A4139 on your left. Turn right up a lane to pass Monkton Priory Church on your right. Go ahead across the B4320 and, passing on old conduit, go up a road which soon deteriorates to a track and leads to Windmill Hill. Converge with a track coming from your right and go ahead to a road.

2. Turn right along the road to Maidenwells. Pass Oxland Park Private Road on your right and turn right where there is a letterbox on the corner, opposite May Cottage, Follow this hedged track.

3. Turn left down a road which soon bears right. Go right at a junction for a quarter of a mile, until the end of woodland on your right and with Orielton Field Centre's entrance on your left.

4. Turn right up a track which leads to the B4320 at Hundleton. Go right a few yards then cross the road and turn sharply left along Guilderoy Road for 50 yards.

5. Fork right down West Grove Lane (a No Through Road). Look out for Coast Path signposts.

6. Fork right along the signposted Coast Path, crossing a stile beside a gate. Pass above a cattery and kennels on your left and go ahead over a stile beside a gate, as signposted, along the right-hand edge of a field. Cross a stream in the corner and climb steps to take a stile into the next field. Reach a lane by crossing a stile in the hedge ahead.

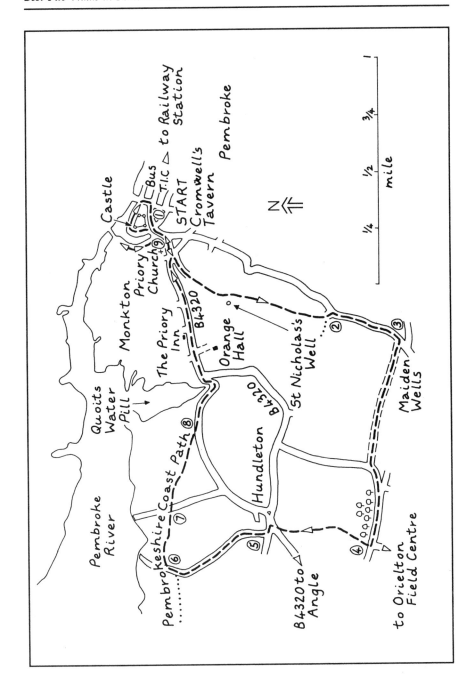

7. Cross the lane and go ahead, as signposted, through a gate. A concrete lane leads to a sewage works. Continue through a kissing-gate along an enclosed path to pass this on your right. Emerge through a second kissing-gate and follow the left-hand edge of the field ahead. Continue over a stile beside a gate and with a hedge on your left. Cross a stone step stile in the wall in the far corner.

8. Bear left, as signposted, down a road. Follow it around Quoits Water Pill to the B4320, where you bear left along the pavement. Pass the entrance to the Orange Hall on your right and the Priory Inn on your left.

9. Approach Pembroke Castle and turn left to gain a view of it from across an arm of the river. Continue towards the castle and fork left around the foot of it, with the water now on your left. Turn right up Northgate, away from the bridge, to turn right and find Cromwell's Tavern on your left, opposite the castle entrance.

26. Manorbier

Route: Manorbier – Pembrokeshire Coast Path – Swanlake Bay -East Moor – Manorbier.

Distance: 3$^1/_2$ miles. Strenuous.

Maps: OS Pathfinder 1125 (Manorbier & Tenby).

Start: The Castle Inn, Manorbier (SS 067978).

Access: Manorbier is on the B4585 about six miles west of Tenby and a similar distance east of Pembroke. Trains from Pembroke and Tenby, Carmarthen, Swansea and Cardiff serve Manorbier station, located just over one mile to the north of the village. Buses (numbers 358 and 359) stop near the Castle Inn on their way between Haverfordwest, Pembroke, Tenby and Carmarthen.

The Castle Inn, Manorbier (0834 871268)

This is the original village pub and full of atmosphere. Highly recommended by the experts, it serves real ale and food and has a beer garden. Opening hours are 11 am to 11 pm on weekdays, noon to 3 pm and 7 pm to 10.30 pm on Sundays. The television version of *The Lion, the Witch and the Wardrobe* and other tales of Narnia were filmed at the nearby castle and the television stars supped here of an evening.

Manorbier Castle

This impressive, well-preserved, fortress was the birth-place of Giraldus Cambrensis around 1146. This cleric and chronicler is best remembered for his *Journey Through Wales*, an account of a preaching tour undertaken with Archbishop Baldwin in 1188 to gain Welsh support for the Third Crusade. It is now available as a Penguin Classic, together with his *Description of Wales*. He declared that he was 'Sprung from the Princes of Wales and from the Barons of the Marches'. Loyal to both sides, when he saw an injustice in either race, he hated it. His grandfather and father were Normans, while his grandmother was the beautiful and amorous 'Helen of Wales', Nest, the daughter of Rhys ap Tewdwr, the last Welsh ruler of Dyfed. As well as the castle, there are a nearby dovecote and mill, while the church across the valley is dedicated to St James the Great. Gerald (Giraldus) had no doubt that this was 'the pleasantest spot in Wales'. The castle is usually open in the summer between 10.30 am and 5.30 pm (admission charge).

Manorbier Castle

The Walk

1. Go left, bear left at a fork and follow the road towards the sea. Pass below Manorbier Castle on your right. Notice the church with its distinctive tower across the valley on your left. Pass a car park with public toilets on your left. Follow the road as it bears right to cross a stream and climb to another car park overlooking Manorbier Bay.

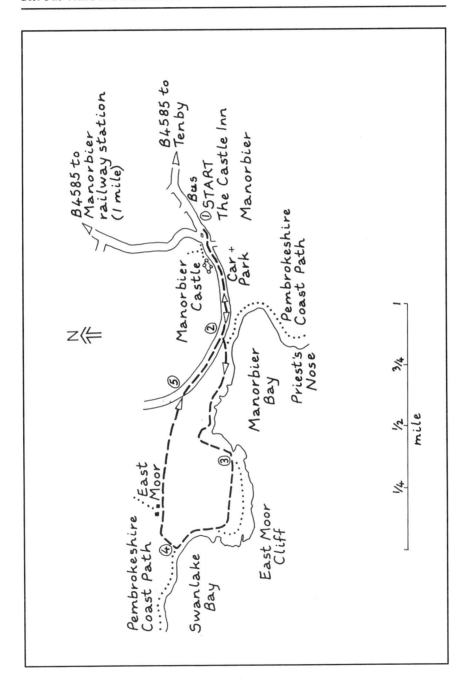

2. Bear left from the road to walk along the Coast Path, keeping the sea on your left.

3. The official Coast Path and the right of way takes a narrow path along the side of the cliff which is overgrown by gorse in places and is not for those of a nervous disposition. A popular unofficial path forks right along the crest of the cliff which is safer and more enjoyable. Descend eventually to Swanlake Bay.

4. After crossing the second stile above the beach of Swanlake Bay, turn right for a vigorous climb uphill to a stile in the fence on your right, at the top. Without crossing it, go inland, to walk with a fence on your right. Turn right, as waymarked, over a step stile in what is now a wall. Follow a hedge on your left to East Moor. Pass the buildings on your left and go ahead over the signposted stone stile to walk along the left-hand edge of three fields.

5. Turn right along the road back into Manorbier, retracing your steps past the car park to the Castle Inn.

27. Tenby

Route: Tenby — Tenby Railway Station — Scotsborough House - Waterwynch — Tenby.

Distance: 6 miles. Moderate.

Map: Either OS Pathfinder 1104 (Tenby) or 1125 (Manorbier & Tenby).

Start: Hope and Anchor, Tenby (SS 136004).

Access: Tenby is on the railway between Carmarthen and Pembroke (start this walk from the railway station at direction point 3). Tenby can also be reached by buses numbers 351 (from Amroth), 352 (from Kilgetty), 358 and 359 (from Haverfordwest or Carmarthen) and 381 (Narberth).

Hope and Anchor, Tenby (0834 842131)

Real ale and food are available in this cosy pub, which has a beer garden and a top deck for children. Self-catering flats are also available, while Nelson and Lady Hamilton stayed in the house across the road in 1802, accompanied by the 29 year old Lady Hamilton's 72 years old husband (Nelson was 44). It was recorded that 'Nelson and Emma walked together evidently vain of each other, while poor Sir William (Hamilton), wretched, but not abashed, followed at a short distance'. The opening hours in this old pub are 11 am to 11 pm on weekdays, noon to 3 pm and 7 pm to 10.30 pm on Sundays.

Tenby

This inviting resort began as a hill fortress, described by a 9th or 10th century Welsh poet as 'a mighty stronghold, sea encircled'. The exciting castle dates from the early years of the Norman invasion. The town walls date from the Middle Ages, giving the feel of a garrison town. The troops must have enjoyed the local beaches and the view across to Caldey Island, with its monastery (boat trips are possible in the summer). Fish were also plentiful in the sea here, earning Tenby's Welsh name of *Dinbych-Y-Pysgod* (Little Fort of the fish). The great scholar Robert Record was born here in 1519 and went onto invent the symbols +, – and =.

By 1800, Tenby was an established seaside resort and Nelson paid the town a visit in 1802, accompanied by Lady Hamilton. The famous artist Augustus John was born here in 1878, by which time the railway link had been established for 12 years and visitors were being advised to bathe in swimming costumes and not to climb Castle Hill to gain a sight of naked ladies bathing within the confines of bathing machines. Also, "no gentleman's bathing machines must be placed within 50 yards of a lady's machine", while "no boat shall come within 100 yards of any bathing machine when used for bathing". Excursion steamers linked Tenby with Ilfracombe and by the 1930s even mixed bathing was tolerated.

Resist the temptations of the beaches for long enough to visit the Tudor Merchant's House (a National Trust Property) on Quay Hill and Tenby Museum, on Castle Hill. This contains painting by Augustus John and is open through the year on weekdays, plus Sundays from Easter to October.

The ruined Scotsborough House passed on this walk just before direction point 6 was a mansion and home of the Ap Rees family. Small boats reached it at high tide before the old estuary was sealed from the sea.

The Walk

1. Go right along St Julian's Street until the Buccaneer Inn on your right. Turn left here down Cobb Lane (for South Beach). Go left along Cresswell Street and The Paragon, keeping the sea and the enticing vision of Caldey Island on your left. Emerge through a gate in the old town wall and bear left with the Esplanade.

2. Go ahead as signposted for the South Beach but soon turn right, inland, as signposted for the station. Go down Queen's Parade, fork left, then right along Station Road to Tenby railway station.

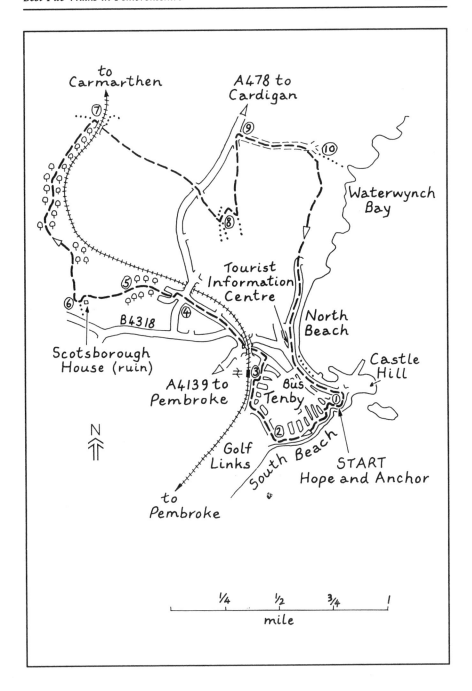

to
Carmarthen

A478 to
Cardigan

⑦

⑨

⑩

Waterwynch
Bay

⑧

Tourist
Information
Centre

⑤

⑥

B4318

North
Beach

④

Scotsborough
House (ruin)

A4139 to
Pembroke

③

Bus

Tenby

Castle
Hill

①

②

N
⇑

Golf
Links

South Beach

START
Hope and Anchor

to
Pembroke

¼   ½   ¾   1

mile

3. Turn right along Warren Street, pass Clement Terrace on your left, then turn left along Greenhill Avenue. Pass the library, then turn left down Greenhill Road and fork right down a path as you approach the railway viaduct. Pass under it and bear right to pass a garage and a road transport workshop on your left. Bear right at a fork and pass the Paddock leading to Jubilee Cottages on your right.

4. Cross the road at the top of the hill and go straight ahead down Lamack Vale. Take a turning on your left and, as the estate road starts to swing right, turn right down a narrow public footpath past the backs of houses. Descend to a stile, cross it and a subsequent stream to take the waymarked path ahead through woodland. Bear left with this path, then climb to a waymarked stile in the top fence.

5. Cross the stile and follow the path along the upper part of the field ahead. Continue through a gate and walk with a hedge on your right at the top of the next field. The track leads on past trees and the remains of Scotsborough House on your left.

6. Turn right through a muddy passage which soon goes right as a distinct, if muddy, path. Eventually reach woodland, which is entered by a waymarked stile. Follow the woodland path until it turns right towards an arched route under the railway.

7. Pass under the railway, ignore a path going to your left and climb with an old green lane ahead. This becomes a metalled lane and takes you to the A478 road. Cross this to take the track opposite.

8. Turn left along the signposted bridleway, ignoring signposted public footpaths on either side. Turn right at the next signpost and converge with another track. Turn sharply left with this, uphill. Return to the A478 and go right for a few yards.

9. Turn right down a private road but public footpath signposted for Waterwynch House Hotel and Bay. Bear right at a fork to take the signposted Coast Path.

10. Turn right uphill along the Coast Path to Tenby. Pass steps going down to the North Beach on your left, then the Tourist Information Centre on your right. Fork left along Crackwell Street to pass above the harbour. Continue with Bridge Street to Castle Square, where you

could bear left to visit Worms Head, Castle Hill, the museum and the castle ruins. Go right along St Julian's Street to return to the Hope and Anchor, on your right.

The old green lane, north of the ruins of Scotsborough House

The next two pages are reserved for your notes as you complete "Best Pub Walks in Pembrokeshire". If you encounter any problems with the walks, please photocopy these pages and send them to us so that we can consider revisions for future editions.

Walking Notes

Route   *Date walked*   *Comments*

Walking Notes

Route   *Date walked*   *Comments*

We publish a wide range of other titles, including general interest publications, guides to individual towns, and books for outdoor activities centred on walking and cycling in the great outdoors throughout England and Wales. This is a recent selection:

Cycling with Sigma ...

CYCLE UK! The Essential Guide to Leisure Cycling
—Les Lumsdon *(£9.95)*

OFF-BEAT CYCLING & MOUNTAIN BIKING IN THE PEAK DISTRICT
—Clive Smith *(£6.95)*

MORE OFF-BEAT CYCLING IN THE PEAK DISTRICT
—Clive Smith *(£6.95)*

50 BEST CYCLE RIDES IN CHESHIRE
—edited by Graham Beech *(£7.95)*

CYCLING IN THE LAKE DISTRICT
—John Wood *(£7.95)*

CYCLING IN SOUTH WALES
—Rosemary Evans *(£7.95)*

CYCLING IN THE COTSWOLDS
—Stephen Hill *(£7.95)*

BY-WAY BIKING IN THE CHILTERNS
—Henry Tindell *(£7.95)*

Country Walking ...

RAMBLES IN NORTH WALES – Roger Redfern
HERITAGE WALKS IN THE PEAK DISTRICT – Clive Price
EAST CHESHIRE WALKS – Graham Beech
WEST CHESHIRE WALKS – Jen Darling

WEST PENNINE WALKS – Mike Cresswell

STAFFORDSHIRE WALKS – Les Lumsdon

NEWARK AND SHERWOOD RAMBLES – Malcolm McKenzie

NORTH NOTTINGHAMSHIRE RAMBLES – Malcolm McKenzie

RAMBLES AROUND NOTTINGHAM & DERBY – Keith Taylor

RAMBLES AROUND MANCHESTER – Mike Cresswell

WESTERN LAKELAND RAMBLES – Gordon Brown *(£5.95)*

WELSH WALKS: Dolgellau and the Cambrian Coast
– Laurence Main and Morag Perrott *(£5.95)*

WELSH WALKS: Aberystwyth and District
– Laurence Main and Morag Perrott *(£5.95)*

WEST PENNINE WALKS – Mike Cresswell

CHALLENGING WALKS IN NORTH-WEST BRITAIN – Ron Astley *(£9.95)*

WALKING PEAKLAND TRACKWAYS – Mike Cresswell *(£7.95)*

– all of the above books are currently £6.95 each, except where indicated

If you enjoy walking 'on the level', be sure to read:

MOSTLY DOWNHILL, Leisurely Walks in the Lake District

MOSTLY DOWNHILL, Leisurely Walks in the White Peak

MOSTLY DOWNHILL, Leisurely Walks in the Dark Peak

Easy, enjoyable walking books; all £6.95

Long-distance walks:

For long-distance walks enthusiasts, we have several books including:

THE GREATER MANCHESTER BOUNDARY WALK – Graham Phythian

THE THIRLMERE WAY – Tim Cappelli

THE FURNESS TRAIL – Tim Cappelli

THE MARCHES WAY – Les Lumsdon

THE TWO ROSES WAY – Peter Billington, Eric Slater,
Bill Greenwood and Clive Edwards

THE RED ROSE WALK – Tom Schofield

FROM WHARFEDALE TO WESTMORLAND:
Historical walks through the Yorkshire Dales – Aline Watson

THE WEST YORKSHIRE WAY – Nicholas Parrott

– all £6.95 each

The Best Pub Walks!

Sigma publish the widest range of "Pub Walks" guides, covering just about every popular walking destination in England and Wales. Each book includes 25–30 interesting walks and varied suitable for individuals or family groups. *The walks are based on "Real Ale" inns of character and are all accessible by public transport.*

Areas covered include

Cheshire • Dartmoor • Exmoor • Isle of Wight • Yorkshire Dales • Peak District • Lake District • Cotswolds • Mendips • Cornwall • Lancashire • Oxfordshire • Snowdonia • Devon

... and dozens more – all £6.95 each!

General interest:

THE INCREDIBLY BIASED BEER GUIDE – Ruth Herman
This is the most comprehensive guide to Britain's smaller breweries and the pubs where you can sample their products. Produced with the collaboration of the Small Independent Brewers' Association and including a half-price subscription to The Beer Lovers' Club. *£6.95*

DIAL 999 – EMERGENCY SERVICES IN ACTION – John Creighton
Re-live the excitement as fire engines rush to disasters. See dramatic rescues on land and sea. Read how the professionals keep a clear head and swing into action. *£9.95*

THE ALABAMA AFFAIR – David Hollett
This is an account of Britain's rôle in the American Civil War. Read how Merseyside dockyards supplied ships for the Confederate navy, thereby supporting the slave trade. The *Alabama* was the most famous of the 'Laird Rams', and was chased half way across the world before being sunk ignominiously. *£9.95*

PEAK DISTRICT DIARY – Roger Redfern
An evocative book, celebrating the glorious countryside of the Peak District. The book is based on Roger's popular column in *The Guardian* newspaper and is profusely illustrated with stunning photographs. *£6.95*

I REMAIN, YOUR SON JACK – J. C. Morten (edited by Sheila Morten)
A collection of almost 200 letters, as featured on BBC TV, telling the moving story of a young soldier in the First World War. Profusely illustrated with contemporary photographs. *£8.95*